# Sex Begins in the Kitchen

# Dr. Kevin Leman

# Sex Begins in the Kitchen

## Because Love Is an All-Day Affair

Fleming H. Revell
A Division of Baker Book House Co
Grand Rapids, Michigan 49516

© 1981, 1992, 1999 by Kevin Leman

Published by Fleming H. Revell
a division of Baker Book House Company
P.O. Box 6287, Grand Rapids, MI 49516-6287

Printed in the United States of America

**Library of Congress Cataloging-in-Publication Data**

Leman, Kevin.
    Sex begins in the kitchen : because love is an all-day
affair / Kevin Leman.—2nd ed.
       p.     cm.
    Includes bibliographical references.
    ISBN 0-8007-5709-2 (paper)
    1. Sex in marriage. 2. Marriage. I. Title.
HQ734.L385    1999
646.7'8—dc21                          99-22767

For the sake of easier reading, the pronouns *he, him,* and *his* refer for the most part to both male and female in the generic sense.

For current information about all releases from Baker Book House, visit our web site:
                  http://www.bakerbooks.com

To my wife, Bucky—
Still my richest blessing

# Contents

# 1

## Why Sex Begins (and Sometimes Ends) in the Kitchen

It's one of those Friday nights when every member of the family has something to do. The two teenagers and their nine-year-old brother are going to the high school football game. It's Dad's night to bowl, and Mom has to go to church to work on decorations for a mother-daughter banquet coming up the following evening. At six-thirty, as soon as dinner is finished, everybody flies out of the house, headed toward their separate destinations.

It's about three hours later when Mom is turning her car into the driveway of her home. She's completely exhausted. It's been a long day, and the only thing she wants to do now is to collapse into bed—but first maybe she'll relax in a tub full of bubbles for a while. And then, as she turns off the ignition and switches off the lights, it hits her: the dishes! She didn't have time to get to the dishes after dinner. In fact, the whole kitchen was a mess.

She thinks for a moment about the possibility of leaving it until morning, but quickly decides that's not possible. Well, so much for her plans for a hot bath and a warm, comfortable bed.

She walks up to the porch, unlocks the front door, tosses her purse on the table in the front hall, and heads straight for the kitchen. Might as well get this out of the way right now.

She stops dead in her tracks as she sees a beautiful, sparkling-clean kitchen. Her first reaction is to think that she got into the neighbor's house by mistake. But she goes back outside, checks the number, and finds that . . . yes, this is her house. She walks back into the house just in time to see her husband hanging up the wet dish towels in the laundry room.

And let me tell you: the guy may have a bald spot on the back of his head, his stomach may hang over his belt—just a little—and he may give the appearance that he's trying hard to grow a second chin. But the old fellow has never looked more desirable to his wife than he does right now.

And that's what I mean when I tell you that sex begins in the kitchen.

Too many people—especially those of us who are fortunate enough to be males—seem to believe that sex begins and ends in the bedroom, period. Some men grunt their way through the evening without showing their wives the least bit of attention. When a man's wife asks him if he thought the dinner she fixed was good, he grunts in response. She tells him about something important that happened to her during the day, and she gets another grunt out of him. She tries to talk to him about something cute that one of the kids did or said and hears the third grunt of the evening. After that, she just gives up trying to talk.

But then when bedtime comes, he's grabbing for her and wondering why she's so "cold" to him. That's just not how "good sex" happens. Sexual intimacy between a man and woman should be the culmination and expression of the intimacy they share in all areas of their life together. For sex to be what it is capable of being, it must be an act of loving and sharing, of giving to each other.

It is most definitely not a game of "I'm Tarzan, you Jane—gimme."

Now before I get myself into trouble, let me explain what I meant a moment ago, about those of us who were "fortunate" enough to be born males. That may have sounded like a sexist statement, but that's definitely not the way I meant it. What I did mean was that as far as I'm concerned, there couldn't be anything better than to be a man who has a deep and abiding relationship with a good woman.

Let me assure you that there have been many times, over the course of the years, when I have thanked the Lord above that he made me a man. And all of those times have had to do with my relationship with my wonderful wife, Sande.

When a man has the deepest sort of communion with a woman who is warm and wonderful and wise—well, he's really got something. My purpose in writing this book is to help men discover that sort of relationship with the women in their lives, and to help women find that sort of relationship with their men.

Let's go back for a moment to the story I told you at the beginning of this chapter.

If you're a woman, chances are that when I got to the part about the dishes having been washed and the kitchen cleaned up, you said something like, "Oh. I thought this was a *true* story."

Or if you're a man, you might have said, "You mean the guy did the dishes? What a wuss!"

Well, guys, if you really want to be macho, if you want to be the virile manly sort of man every woman wants . . .

11

then you'd be wise to tie on an apron once in a while and take a couple of steps in the direction of dishpan hands.

I talked to a woman once who told me she was seriously thinking about leaving her husband. She said he was insensitive and thoughtless and never seemed to take her feelings into consideration.

Everything had come to a head for her one night when she had been gone for a couple of hours to an open house at their daughter's school. She had tried to talk him into going with her, but he couldn't see the importance of getting to know their little girl's teachers, nor talking to them about how she was progressing with her schoolwork.

She wanted to fix something quick for supper, so she grilled some hamburgers. But, as in my opening story, she didn't have time to clean things up before she left for the meeting. When she got home later that evening, her husband was slouched in his favorite chair, watching a lumberjack competition on one of the sports channels. He didn't even turn around and acknowledge her as she came through the door. He didn't ask her how the evening had been, or simply say, "Hi, hon. I'm glad you're home."

Then she walked into the dining room.

Not only had her husband not done the dishes—he hadn't made a single move toward straightening anything up. The lids hadn't been put back on the mustard or the mayonnaise. In fact, the mayonnaise had a knife resting in it. Nothing had been put back in the refrigerator—including a half gallon of milk, which was now room temperature. The slices of cheese were still on a plate, as were the leaves of lettuce, slices of tomato, and some grated onions. Add a couple of wadded-up napkins for good measure, and you've got the picture.

The wife was angry enough that she made a little bit of noise putting things away. She didn't confront her husband, but he must have heard her banging the refrigerator door a few times and clanging the silverware unnecessarily as she carried it into the kitchen. But he didn't respond.

By the time she was finished, she couldn't wait to get into bed. She was so tired.

And, of course, she was still angry too, so she pulled the covers up around her chin and made sure she was lying on her half of the bed. And you know what happened? Her husband came in fifteen or twenty minutes later, climbed into bed, snuggled up against her, and then reached over and put his hand on her breast—as if that were supposed to make her wild with desire. It didn't. He might as well have been trying to heat an entire office building with the flame from one cigarette lighter.

And when his wife didn't respond, he tried to sweet talk her by using those six words every woman wants to hear, "Geez—what's the matter with you?"

For some reason, this lady decided to stay with the guy. She said she "loved him," even though she wasn't really sure why. But if the story she told me was typical of what goes on in many homes across America, then there are a great many people who need to be brought to the understanding that sex really does begin in the kitchen— and it's to these people that this book is dedicated.

Now, admittedly, the example I've just given is pretty extreme. Maybe your marriage isn't that bad. I *hope* it isn't that bad. But maybe there are some difficulties that you'd like to work out, some ways in which the communication between the two of you isn't as good as it could be. If so, then this book is for you too. I'll tell you how you can go about establishing or repairing communication within your marriage.

*Sex Begins in the Kitchen* is premised on the idea that your mate ought to be the number-one priority in your life; that a good marital relationship is based upon pleasing each other, being sensitive and tuned-in to each other's

13

emotional—as well as sexual—needs. This book concerns itself with our need to be intimate with each other as husband and wife; to share our most intimate thoughts and feelings; to understand the different languages in which we express our love; to come together as one in marriage, both emotionally and physically.

Unfortunately, in most marriages, couples seem to live in a "married-singles" lifestyle. In too many of these homes nothing at all happens behind bedroom doors. And if a sexual relationship does exist, it occurs only as a ritual or a duty, a few minutes squeezed in after the late news and before Letterman.

It is hardly the culmination of an entire day full of affection, consideration, love, and oneness.

Now this isn't to say that on that Friday night when Dad did the dishes before Mom got home he was going to be rewarded with a sexual encounter with his wife. However, Mom's feelings when she walked into the house and saw what her husband had done had to be, "Hey! What a neat experience to walk in and find that he beat me home by a half hour and was thoughtful enough to clean the kitchen!" He was showing his wife that he loved her and not doing it because he was thinking, "Hey . . . maybe she'll make love to me if she sees that I did the dishes."

Motivation is important here as in every other area of life. False motives will be spotted a mile or more away, but acts done out of the motivation of love will produce dividends in all areas of your life together as husband and wife. What the husband in my illustration has done is an act of love toward his wife as surely as anything else he's ever done for her—and it lets her know that she is important enough to him that he will do what he can to make life more pleasurable for her. This kind of consideration in your own marriage can do nothing but bring you closer together as man and wife.

What will it take to get your marriage to the place where the primary motivation for all the interaction between you and your mate is love? What can you do to correct some of the problem areas that may now exist?

Throughout this book, I will share with you some of the things I have discovered during my years of experience as a marriage and family counselor and psychologist and, more importantly, during my years as a husband and father. I have watched thousands of couples come to grips with the fact that they have to open up and take a good look at themselves in order to have a satisfying marriage. Most of us don't really understand ourselves. But if you are going to share with your mate and become one in marriage, you must be able to recognize your own feelings—why you do what you do, what preconditioning you have received, and so on. You have to see how these influences have affected your way of thinking and be able to "reprogram" yourself in the places where you need it.

You also need to know what it means to be committed to making whatever changes are needed in your own behavior.

And that's important. If you want to change somebody else's behavior, the best thing you can do is to change your own behavior first. Handing your husband a book and saying, "Here, George, I think you ought to read this," won't do you any good.

Telling your wife, "You know, I've been reading about the importance of good communication in marriage, and you really could do a better job," isn't going to win her over to your way of thinking. But if you demonstrate by your own actions that you want to make things better between you—if you'll begin doing those little things to show your mate how much you care—then I can almost guarantee that you're going to see a steady improvement in your marriage.

Now let's take a quick look at what lies ahead:

- In the chapter titled "The Plight of Marriage," I will discuss why most marriages are in trouble, so that you can recognize some warning signs in your own.
- In the chapter "Whom Did You Marry?" you will see the big part that your birth order and your mate's birth order play in your marriage.
- In "Making the Pieces Fit," we'll talk about the fact that you can never change another person, but that you must effect changes within yourself based solely on your own desire to change. But I'll tell you how you can *allow* your mate to change by changing your own behavior.
- "One Plus One Equals One" will discuss the importance of being able to express your innermost thoughts and feelings to your mate—and . . .
- "Nothing More Than Feelings" will continue this process.
- In "Women Are from Pluto and Men Are a Bit Goofy Too," we'll discuss the different needs of men and women. You can't expect your spouse to need the same things you need from your marriage.
- "Dr. Leman, You're Overdrawn" blends two extremely helpful concepts from other authors—Willard Harley's "Love Bank" and Gary Chapman's "Love Languages." You and your spouse probably express your love in different ways. If you never learn to "interpret" these "love languages," you'll never be sure how much love is getting across to the other person.
- "How to Be Good and Angry" will tell you how to deal with anger and frustration.
- Another chapter, "Games Couples Play," will tell you about some dangerous and destructive games that

married men and women play with each other—and I'm not talking about party games. In one of the sections of that chapter, Children Are the Enemy, I will tell you how to stop letting those cute little "spittin' images" of yourselves come between you and your spouse.

- "Ying-Yangs, Weenies, Tallywackers, and 'The Thing'" is a real eye-opener on sexual relationships. I have discovered that most men haven't taken the time to understand their wives at all, which leads to an unfulfilling sexual relationship for both of them.

- And finally, "Couples of Promise" challenges you to make Ten Commitments to preserve and improve your marriage. Will you take the ideas of this book and actually apply them to your life together, or just leave them on these pages?

So . . . that's what's in store for you as you go through the rest of *Sex Begins in the Kitchen.*

You know, one of the things that really troubles me about many of my colleagues in the discipline of psychology is that they promote the notion that men and women are really the same—that the differences between us are physical and nothing more.

Well . . . 'tain't true.

Men and women are different. If you are a woman, you are female in every aspect of your life. Being a woman doesn't mean that you wear your hair long and are partial to blouses and skirts. Everything you do and experience in life is filtered through the fact of your sexuality, whether you are female or male.

Are the sexes equal? Absolutely. But they are not the same. A happy marriage is one in which both partners understand and accept those differences, and understand how to relate to each other *in spite* of the fact that they relate to the world differently. The key to growth and enrichment in marriage is in reaching out and being able to touch each other in a special way that conveys, "I understand how you feel and I'm going to do my very best to meet your needs."

I'm sure you know the statistic, that nearly 50 percent of all marriages in the United States end in divorce. It shouldn't be that way, it doesn't have to be that way, and *Sex Begins in the Kitchen* is aimed at putting a dent in that "unsuccess" rate.

You probably are reading this book for one of several reasons: Maybe you want a more satisfying marriage. Or perhaps your marriage is in trouble and you want to do what you can to save it. Or maybe you are planning to marry soon and you want to do what you can to make sure you don't show up as a negative statistic at some point in the future.

Well, I may not have the answer to every single issue and/or question that arises between a husband and wife, but I guarantee you that *Sex Begins in the Kitchen* will be practical and will give you some guidelines and insights into turning your relationship around and making your marriage what it should be.

But keep in mind that just reading this book will not be enough to help you. The important part is putting it into practice, making it all a part of your daily life. For that reason, I urge you to view this as a textbook of sorts. If you come across something you believe to be particularly applicable to your situation, highlight it, put an asterisk by it, or do whatever you need to do to get it to soak in. If you find something you don't like, or that you don't believe applies to you, cross it out or rip it out of the book. I won't mind. My experience tells me that all of the principles in this book are valid, but not every principle will apply to every reader—and besides, my words are not carved in stone.

In many of the chapters I will include exercises for you to do that will reinforce what I've been saying. This is because it is *action* that will bring about the needed changes in any situation or relationship—and I know that these exercises will enable you to better understand how to incorporate into your own life the principles and suggestions found within this book.

I will also include a number of examples based on couples I have counseled. Again, it is easier to see how principles will work if you can see how they worked in the lives of others. Some of the case histories we're going to talk about may prompt a flicker of recognition, and others may seem rather extreme. But in every situation, my desire is for you to see how what worked for someone else might also be applied in your own life.

Before moving on, I want to tell you a couple of things about sex and marriage that I strongly believe in:

Sex belongs in marriage.
Sex belongs *only* in marriage.

Let me explain.

First of all, when I say that sex belongs in marriage, I mean that the sexual union is a vital part of the love that brought a man and woman together as husband and wife in the first place. A while ago I was flipping channels and came across a talk show where several married couples were talking about how happy they were to be taking part in the "new celibacy." Some of them hadn't made love in several years, and they seemed to be happy as clams about it. (Although I couldn't help but wonder if perhaps a couple of clams wouldn't have had a more exciting life.)

If a healthy man and woman who are husband and wife look me in the eye and tell me they are perfectly happy without any sort of sexual contact between them, my reaction is not, "That's great." My reaction is, "There's something wrong here." The sexual aspect of life is one of the great gifts from our Creator, and long-term celibacy between married couples is simply not normal or healthy, no matter how much it may be considered the "in" thing.

I do not believe that for a marriage to be healthy a husband and wife have to engage in sex five or six times a week—or even once a week. Frequency is entirely up to the couple and should be based on mutual respect and a desire to please the other partner. The couple should come together in this way often enough that they are both fulfilled sexually. Furthermore, the wife needs to know that her husband sees her as sexually desirable, and the husband needs to know that his wife enjoys being with him in this intimate way. In fact, one of the greatest needs of most married men is sexual fulfillment. Notice I didn't say sex. Men need to feel wanted sexually.

And as I mentioned earlier, in order for the sexual relationship to be healthy, all other aspects of the couple's relationship must also be healthy—and it's the purpose of this book to help ensure that they are.

Now, the second point I made is that sex belongs *only* in marriage.

For many Christians this is a no-brainer. But many others would look at me as if I *am* a no-brainer. For centuries Christians and other religious folks have preached the value of fidelity, chastity, and monogamy. But the sexual revolution of our age has made premarital and extramarital dalliances commonplace. For the last couple of decades, whenever I stood up in a public forum and promoted sex only within marriage, I was branded as some sort of religious kook.

But things are changing. More and more, as mental and physical health professionals grapple with the problems brought about by sexual promiscuity—which range from chronic depression all the way to AIDS—even the most libertine people are beginning to see that a lifetime monogamous relationship between one man and one woman is the ideal.

Sometimes I think the world has turned topsy-turvy when I see married couples on television talking about the joys of celibacy, and then I turn the channel and see a drama glorifying sex between two unmarried individuals.

Why do I believe that marriage is the only context in which a sexual relationship should take place?

- First, because I personally believe that's the way we were created. You might say that I believe the "divine plan" is for one man and one woman to pledge their lives to each other, to encourage one another, to support one another, to be totally loyal to each other in all areas of life, including sexuality. The Bible consistently restricts sex to the marriage relationship, and I believe God's laws are perfect. He knew what he was doing when he set up this marriage thing.

- Second, sex is a powerful experience that triggers extremely strong emotions. Some people insist they are immune to those emotions, but the truth is that they aren't. So even from a purely psychological, nonreligious perspective, sex was never meant to be an impersonal act. Like it or not, you become emotionally bonded to your sex partner.

- Third, my feeling is that sex is to be shared only with someone you love deeply, and if you love that person deeply enough to have sex with him or her, then you should also love that person deeply enough to commit your life to him or her through marriage.

- The final reason is simply that promiscuous sex is dangerous—physically, mentally, and emotionally. I love

21

a little verse tucked away in the next to the last book of the Bible. "Stay always within the boundaries where God's love can reach and bless you" (Jude 21 TLB). Sexual fidelity is not a matter of keeping our hands out of some delightful cookie jar. It's about enjoying a full and honest relationship in which God can bless us.

It could be that you have had numerous sexual partners, and if that's the case, I don't want you to think, "Well, I guess this book isn't for me" and put it down. But what I do want is to encourage you to have a new attitude about sex, a new respect for it that sees it as something more than fun, or more than something you do to get attention. After all, the whole intent here is to replace those old destructive or harmful patterns and attitudes with new ones that are constructive and beneficial.

There are many reasons why I like being a psychologist. But one of the things I like most about it is that I often get to play a part in restoring a relationship between a husband and wife. I like nothing better than seeing a man and woman holding hands in my office, or exchanging loving glances with each other, when a few weeks or months earlier they didn't even want to be in the same room.

Now it's not always easy to effect that sort of change in a relationship. Sometimes it takes many months, and sometimes it doesn't happen at all. Yes, I admit to having lost a few—but that's almost always been because one or both partners refused to make the changes that were necessary to restore their marriage.

I honestly believe that if you and your spouse (or future spouse) will commit yourselves to each other, and will implement many of the ideas I express in *Sex Begins in the Kitchen,* chances are very good that you are going to be richly blessed by a beautiful marriage.

Again, it isn't always easy. The road isn't always down-hill with the wind blowing at your back. There are going to be some low spots along the way, as well as some highs. But with commitment to each other, each blessing and each drawback can only succeed in bringing greater under-standing and fulfillment to your marriage.

Are you and your spouse reading this book together? It wouldn't be a bad idea. Maybe you could read a chapter a night in bed or after dinner. Or leave it around the house with two bookmarks (his and hers). Schedule time to talk about what you're reading, and to put into practice the suggestions at the end of each chapter.

# 2

## The Plight of Marriage

The young lawyer was having a rough day of it. As she typed up her notes, her fingers just weren't hitting the correct letters. She lost track of an important document and accidentally dropped her cell phone in the trash.

"What's the matter with you?" her partner teased. "Are you in love or something?"

"Of course I'm not in love," she snapped back. "I'm married."

It's sad, but it's true, that we often think of marriage and love as having precious little to do with each other, or even as being contradictions in terms.

It's like what happened when a boy was asked by one of his neighbors, "Is your sister still dating that nice young man? They always seemed to be so much in love."

"Not anymore," he replied. "They hardly even talk to each other these days."

"Oh," said the neighbor lady, "I'm so sorry to hear they broke up."

"They didn't break up," the boy told her. "They got married."

Again, that's the way we often think of marriage, isn't it? If you want to take the romance out of a relationship, run out and get a marriage license. It's almost as if there's something magical about a wedding ring. Slip it on the finger of someone you love, and all the romance evaporates into thin air.

The stand-up comedian Henny Youngman made a living with his famous line, "Take my wife—please." He had his audiences in stitches because they knew exactly what he meant.

It's been quite a few years since Carly Simon had a hit song with "That's the Way I've Always Heard It Should Be," but it still stands out as a picture of the negative way some people think about marriage.

In her song, Carly Simon draws a dark and unhappy picture of married life—her father sitting all alone in the dark, smoking his cigarette; her mother in her bedroom, reading her magazine all by herself, nothing better to do with her time. The mother and father never touch, never speak, never show any sort of love for each other.

The song is prompted by the question, "Will you marry me?" and the singer is not responding positively, because when she looks at her parents she believes that this is the sort of thing marriage does to people.

And if you watch TV much, you might get the same idea of marriage from a number of modern programs—*Married with Children,* for instance, or *The Simpsons.* On the screen, marriage seldom seems fulfilling. It's a battleground, a swamp of dissatisfaction. Even the shows that offer a more positive glimpse of married life—*Home Improvement* or *Mad About You*—regularly find mirth in marital misfortune. Complaints are comical. Bliss is boring.

What do you think? What's your image of married life? Do you go along with Carly Simon's haunting song—that the way you've always heard it should be is pretty dismal? Does marriage turn people into dolts and dingbats, as the TV sitcoms tell us?

Unfortunately, the answer is yes . . . sometimes. Many married couples do live that sort of life—but it doesn't have to be that way—not at all.

Why are so many marriages in trouble? Well, there are a number of factors that have contributed to marriage being in its present level of decay—and before we move on I want to talk about a few of these.

## SOCIAL TURMOIL

The very foundations of marriage have been weakened during the past several decades by social turmoil, a series of democratic revolutions within our country and the world at large.

Don't misunderstand and think I'm saying that these revolutions were bad. I'm not one of those who longs for the good old days, when everyone knew his or her place in society, and no one would think of speaking out against the status quo.

But at the same time, even though these events in general have been necessary and positive, there have been some misapplications and misunderstandings that have harmed the institution of marriage.

It used to be that men were looked upon as being superior somehow to women, that fair-skinned people were better than those with dark skin, and that adults were better than children. But today we've come to understand that people are equal regardless of their gender, skin color, or age.

That's good, but it also means that those who once thought of themselves as better have had to redefine their understanding of their roles in society. For example, as women began to assert themselves and demand equality in the eyes of their husbands and other men, their husbands became confused and insecure. A husband didn't know how to handle this woman, who was definitely not "like the girl who married dear old Dad."

These changes have had an adverse effect on marriage, the home, and sexual relationships. In many instances, the man has become defensive and threatened by his wife's independence and drive for equality. He wants to take care of her, to protect her, and it is hard for him to deal with a woman who doesn't think she needs to be protected.

There has always been something within the nature of man that makes him think of himself as the knight—the one who has to kill the dragon to rescue the fair damsel. Is that all baloney? No, I believe those feelings were put within man for a purpose. Whereas I believe that men and women are absolute equals, I also believe that men are naturally physically stronger than women.

Yes, I've seen some female bodybuilders, and I wouldn't want to get into an arm-wrestling competition with any of them. But generally speaking, it is the man who is able to get the stuck lid off the mayonnaise jar. Traditionally men have been stronger, and I believe that part of the protective nature of men in general stems from ancient times, when there were dangers on all sides—from wild animals, enemy tribesmen, you name it. In those days, the man was forced into the role of hunter, warrior, and protector, and it's something that is still within most of us—to some degree at least—today.

You may know that I live in the foothills of the Arizona desert. Because of this, we frequently see quail run up out of the wash behind our house and into our backyard. One morning I was sitting at the table with my wife, Sande, having a cup of coffee, when I saw Ma and Pa Quail and several tiny baby quail run into the yard. The little ones darted around all over the place while their mother sort of ran around in circles, looking for all the world like a sheepdog with feathers as she sought to keep her little ones together. The old man didn't seem to be helping very much. Instead, he flew up onto the birdbath, took a little drink of water, and then sat there looking around. Meanwhile, there was Ma, down on her hands and knees, so to speak, with the kids. And I wondered if she was feeling a little bit of anger over the situation—if she wasn't wanting to say something like, "You get down here and give me a hand with these kids!"

But then it hit me that what the father was doing was living out his role within the family. His role demanded that he seek higher ground so that he could see any danger that might be in the area—perhaps a cat looking for a light snack. Like all men everywhere, he was *supposed* to watch for any threat to his family and warn them if he saw something evil headed their way.

You know, of course, that over the last few years there has been much negative publicity about anabolic steroids, which are often taken illegally by some athletes to boost their strength. Steroids used this way are dangerous, and that's why they've been so much in the news—but it's interesting to note that many consist largely of the male hormone testosterone, which tends to make those who take it more aggressive, more combative, and stronger.

To me, that says a great deal about man's natural role as the protector. I don't care how enlightened a man may be, there is still within him that desire to protect his woman. A woman who's intelligent will be aware of that and will not be offended by it.

At the same time, a man who lives in the modern world needs to at least try to understand that his lady-fair may not see herself as a damsel in distress, but as someone who is her husband's equal in every sense of the word.

I have to be careful here, because I don't want anyone to misunderstand and think that I'm against the changes that have taken place in society. That's not it at all. It's sad that we ever had such ideas about superiority and inferiority. Many times, poor sexual relationships between husband and wife are premised on superior-inferior relationships, where somebody is assumed to be better than somebody else.

If you go into a marriage assuming that you are up here and your wife is down there in the pits somewhere, you're going to lose. You just can't win in that posture.

I'll say it again in case you didn't hear me the first time— men and women are absolute equals.

But that doesn't mean we're the same—and I don't know about you, but I'm mighty glad that we're not! Physically, mentally, and emotionally, males and females were made to complement each other. The problem is that neither men nor women have known how to handle the changes in traditional positions that have taken place within our society, and that's why the social upheaval in our society has contributed to the turmoil in marriage.

## INADEQUATE MODELS

Another reason why the negative view of marriage is so often true is that children model what they've learned from their parents. In other words, many people don't know what it means to have a good marriage because they've never seen one.

I remember a man who couldn't understand why his marriage was in trouble—especially after he had been such a good and faithful husband.

"Doc, I'm telling you," he said, "I've been a good husband. I bet I haven't had more than eight other women in the thirteen years we've been married."

The tragedy of this was that Ron was really serious. He thought he was being a good husband and father by limiting himself to less than one extramarital sexual encounter per year. He wasn't setting a very good example for his children to follow, and I couldn't help but wonder what sort of example his father had set for him.

I can't help but think of Bill Clinton, whose own family was rather unstable as he grew up. In his adult life, he has engaged in at least a few extramarital affairs, perhaps many. His boyhood idol was John F. Kennedy, whose own sexual appetite has more recently come to light. In fact, from everything I have read, most of the Kennedy brothers regarded women as sexual playthings—and that's something they learned from *their* father.

Make no mistake: Children learn about marriage from their parents and other role models. I worry about today's children: what they've learned from President Clinton's example. His own wife wrote that "it takes a village to raise a child," and sadly, she's finding that it takes a village to keep an eye on her husband—perhaps a whole country! All politics aside, we need leaders in every facet of life who set examples with their strong marriages. Yet the most important leaders of all are parents.

We are now seeing a whole generation, age zero to about thirty, that has grown up in an age of divorce and sexual experimentation. Some have seen their parents modeling marital fidelity and stability. Many haven't. Is it any wonder that they have such a negative view of marriage?

Children really do model what they see.

I got a firsthand look at the truth of this when my son, Kevin II, was no more than two years old. I was driving down a city street, with Kevin in the seat next to me, when I decided that I needed to roll down the window so I could—of all things—spit. I had no sooner spit out the window when I caught one on the side of my neck from my son. Who says that children don't model our behavior!

And the lesson I learned that day went much further than "be careful where and when you spit."

When a little boy grows up in a home where his father treats his mother like trash, chances are he'll grow up to treat his own wife like trash. If a little girl sees her mother running around on her father and making him look like a fool at every opportunity, she will come to think of her own sexuality in terms of conquering men in this way.

It's a sad truth that too many married people use each other. Women use men as providers, as escorts, as disciplinarians. Men use women, making them feel like nothing more than sexual receptacles, like objects. I once counseled a young woman who had had so many sexual partners she couldn't remember them all. And yet she had never once experienced any sort of satisfaction. She told me that she was tired of feeling like a receptacle, but that's all she knew how to be, because that's what she had learned from the relationship between her mother and father.

If a young boy never sees a caring, loving father who meets the needs of his wife and children on a daily basis, but rather sees his dad continually dump on his mom, then he will deduce that women are for using and will select someone whom he can use. Or a young woman may feel that the only role she can perform satisfactorily is the role of mother and homemaker because her mother taught her that women are acceptable only in this situation. She may want desperately to be a doctor or lawyer, but she can't do it because she believes that those things are not open to females. Or at least females like her.

I recently saw a film of what happened when a monkey was taken out of its cage at a zoo and turned loose to play in a nearby pasture. Every couple of feet that monkey would thrust his body forward as if to jump from bar to bar—even though there were no bars to swing from or to. He was demonstrating learned behavior that he had incorporated over the past fifteen years. The behavior was so ingrained in the monkey's life that it was difficult for him to behave in any other way. Changing his environment didn't change his personality. And we human beings are very much like that monkey. Just because we grow up, it doesn't mean that negative behavior will cease. The behavior is usually so ingrained that it follows us into adulthood. Chances are we still use the basic behavior we once exhibited.

Picture these two situations, and then ask yourself how you would react—what it would be like in your house.

Dad comes home after a busy day at the office to find Mom in the kitchen working on dinner. He comes up behind her, gives her a loving pat on the fanny, and then puts his arms around her. Mom doesn't say anything but struggles loose from him, turns, and glares in a way that says, "Do you mind! The children are watching!"

Second situation: Dad's behavior is exactly the same, only this time Mom turns around and gives him a warm welcome-home kiss—right there in front of little Festus and Festina.

Now, in which situation did the children get the wrong message? You know, of course, that it was in the first situation, where Mom was so concerned about doing something "wrong" in front of the kids. In fact, that first reaction was the wrong one—the reaction that says, "There will be no displays of affection in front of the children." You see, children are going to learn from you one way or the other. They may learn that it's okay for a husband and wife to love each other and to treat each other with tenderness and affection—or they may learn that marriage is a battleground. But either way, they will learn.

Recently a book made a case that parents really don't make much of a difference in how their children turn out. Duh. Hello! Did people actually buy this book? Of course, in the same month the government released the results of a $25 million study finding that parents really *do* make a difference. Your tax dollars at work. Hmm. For a measly $3 million or so I could have told them *that*.

But you don't need a multimillion-dollar study to know this. You don't even need this book to tell you. (And you certainly don't need that other book to deny it.) If you have kids, you *know* you're affecting them with everything you do. And even if you don't have kids, you know how your folks affected *you*, for good or bad.

In many ways, life is like those ads for Fram oil filters. "You can pay me now, or pay me later." But you will eventually have to pay the price for what your parents taught you and for what you are passing along to your children.

Somewhere along the line you may have learned from your parents' example that kissing is bad, that hugging is a no-no, and that sex is something shameful. And that kind of teaching is hard to overcome.

We have virtually no training for the jobs of marriage and parenthood, and that is tragic. I believe that when you are at your worst you are probably being just like your mother or father were when they were at their worst. We've all told ourselves, "I'll never say that to my kids." But then we hear ourselves not only saying the same words our parents said to us, but even using the same voice inflection!

Still, in our parents' day many people were able to keep their marriages together in spite of the problems they faced, just because there was an aversion to divorce. There was an attitude that said, "Our marriage commitment was 'til death do us part, and we both want to honor that. Whatever is wrong between us, we can work it out." But in our less-restrictive society, and because of the increased pressures and demands of modern life, we cannot keep our marriages together without a meaningful precedent and without some outside help.

A friend of mine told me recently that his ten-year-old daughter had discovered that hers was the only family among those of her seven or eight closest friends who still had the "original" Mom and Dad. Forty years ago that would have been considered an incredible statistic. Today it's considered absolutely normal.

Thankfully, some things are beginning to happen that should have a positive effect on the state of marriage within the United States. Marriage and parenting classes are being instituted in some churches and schools, and more and more clergymen are refusing to marry couples who have not gone through premarital counseling. There are also marriage enrichment seminars and organizations such as Marriage Encounter that can help a marriage that is in trouble—and I am delighted to see the work they are doing. There's also a new organization I have founded, Couples of Promise, that's going to teach millions of couples how to become one, how to stay in love. We'll even show single people how to find a "keeper."

Another thing you can do, if you believe that you are someone who had his perception of the husband-wife relationship damaged by inadequate role models, is to begin seeing a competent therapist. But how do you find one?

If you are involved in a church or synagogue, ask your pastor or rabbi if he knows of someone he might recommend. Perhaps he is a qualified marriage counselor himself.

If you seek out professional help, be sure that the therapist you choose is someone who wants to deal with whatever problems you have, give you some direction and alternatives, and then get rid of you as quickly as possible. In other words, don't get locked into a long-term therapeutic marathon that is going to cost you more than you can afford to pay in terms of both time and money. In my own practice, I prefer to see someone for no more than ten sessions, and perhaps even as few as five. It's rare when we can't get a handle on the problem in that amount of time. If your therapist is talking about seventy, eighty, ninety sessions or more over a period of years, you have a right to wonder if he or she is really anxious to get you on the right road or is just interested in buying a new boat on the easy payment plan.

Once you have the names of three or four recommended people, take the time to call and ask some questions, the least of which in terms of importance is "How much do you charge?" You aren't looking for the best price for a lawn sprinkler. You are talking about someone who is going to enter your very private world—a world that is an area that is so vital to your being. To make sure you've found the right person, here are some questions I would suggest that you ask:

1. What values are important in your own life? Do you have faith in God?
2. Are you married? How long have you been married? How many times have you been married?
3. What counseling methods do you employ? Is there one particular model you adhere to? Can you give me a brief explanation?
4. Do you see couples together, individually, or some of each? Do you ever see the entire family?
5. How long should we expect therapy to continue? How many sessions?
6. Will my medical insurance pay for your services? (This question should be directed to your insurance provider as well.)
7. What academic degree(s) do you have? Any postgraduate training?
8. Do you have children? If so, what are their ages?
9. What are your fees? How many minutes in a session?
10. Can I make monthly payments on my account?
11. Are you certified by the State Board of Psychologist Examiners or other appropriate boards? What are your professional affiliations?

## Too-Early Marriages

Many marriages are in trouble today because people marry too young. Although college-educated white-collar professionals are often waiting until they're in their middle or late twenties to get married, teenage weddings are still very common, especially among those who do not plan to go on to college or who are not particularly focused on a career.

Part of the reason for all of these teenage marriages is that the sex drive is extremely high during the late teens for both boys and girls.

Unfortunately, these young people do not have a realistic view of the responsibilities that go along with marriage and parenthood. They are "in love" and that's all that matters. They may not have any money. They may not have the first idea of how to cope with any of the problems life will throw at them. They may not have taken the time to get to know each other—beyond their frequent "wrestling" matches in the backseat of a car or on her living-room sofa. All they know is that they're in love, and love will keep them together.

Whenever I talk to high school students, I try to give them a better understanding of what it means to love someone, and I also tell them that marriage is not all roses and sexual thrills.

I tell them to picture themselves nursing their loved ones through a bout of the flu—complete with the prospect of mopping up the vomit because that loved one couldn't make it to the toilet in time. I talk about pacing the floor at night with a baby who is suffering from diarrhea or an ear infection. I try to get them to realize that they will have to go without things if they have not taken the time to adequately prepare to support a family financially.

I ask questions such as: Do you like movies? Are you prepared to give them up so you can be married? Do you like to go out to a restaurant with a group of friends? Are you prepared to stay home instead and eat peanut butter sandwiches? Are you ready to start spending money on Pampers and formula instead of CDs and rock concerts?

Still, I realize that it's hard to give realistic answers to questions like these when you're in love.

So what can parents do?

Well, for one thing, they can refuse to give in to the unrelenting demands of their teenagers or preteenagers to let them date. The best way to discourage too-early dating is never to encourage it. People frequently ask very young children, in a joking way, "Got a girlfriend [or boyfriend] yet?" Naturally, the child begins to assume this is something that is expected of him. If it is understood from the time your child is very young that he or she can begin dating at the age of sixteen (or whatever age you choose), then he or she already knows the house rules long before the teen years come around.

When I was a boy in elementary school, you couldn't admit that you liked girls, even if you did, because it just wasn't the thing to do. If a girl so much as touched you, you had to make a face and worry about getting cooties. It was the way you were expected to act if you were a "man."

And as far as the girls were concerned, the only thing they seemed to think boys were good for was a good, solid kick in the shins. I remember, back in fourth grade, how the girls used to spend recess chasing the boys all over the school yard. And if one of them caught you, look out, because she wasn't interested in a kiss. Instead, you could count on the fact that you were going to have a couple of very sore shins for a few days! It was the battle of the sexes, and my own shins fell victim to it more than once!

Today, though, young boys and girls feel pressure to show interest in the opposite sex whether they're really interested or not. From early ages, they're bombarded with sexual images in the media—sex is what grown-ups do, and all kids want to grow up. We adults don't help matters any by asking little boys, "Do you have a girlfriend yet?" In some cases, sexual interest becomes a matter of identity. Kids feel they need to prove their heterosexuality, or at least their social value. In many high schools (and some junior highs), kids are ashamed to admit they're virgins.

It's hard to overcome peer pressure, but it is absolutely essential that parents let their children know—again and again—that it doesn't matter what anyone else says about you. The important thing is that you are true to yourself, and that you behave in the way you know to be correct.

Unfortunately, another reason for so many teenage marriages is that parents make home life so miserable for their children that any situation looks better than the one he or she is in at the present. Any outreach of "love" is grabbed at without thinking for a moment about the consequences.

For example, I remember Marty and Denise, who came to me when they were twenty-two and twenty-one. Marty was brought up in a permissive home where he was given far too many freedoms as a child and very few responsibilities. Denise, on the other hand, grew up in a home where there was a very poor marriage. Just before the time she met Marty, when she was fourteen, her parents had gone through a rough divorce. To complicate matters for her, her father was an angry and abusive man.

It wasn't too long after Marty and Denise first began to date that they found themselves in an intimate relationship. They certainly didn't love each other, but at fifteen and fourteen they weren't old enough to know the difference between love and physical infatuation. (Believe me when I tell you that I counsel many people in their thirties and forties who still don't know the difference.) The lack of male attention and love in Denise's home was a factor that led to her involvement with Marty and to her marriage to him when she was only sixteen. She dropped out of school and took a job as a cashier in a grocery store, while Marty got a job as a carpenter's apprentice. Their marriage somehow survived for five years, during which time they had a daughter. But their relationship was pitifully devoid of love, and it had finally become evident that their union was destructive. Now they were beginning to look around them and wonder why their lives were in shambles at such an early age.

Eventually, they decided to go their separate ways.

At times it seems that just about every young couple is living together before marrying. I'm seeing an increasing number of men and women who moved in together one to three years before the wedding, but once they tied the knot, they found the whole relationship quickly unraveling. Why? Because when they were asked to make a real commitment to each other, they had trouble doing it.

In fact, there's some interesting research that shows that living together actually increases the probability of divorce. Sharing the same four walls may *seem* like a commitment, but if you want to break it off, you just have to call a moving van. It *feels* like an intimate step, but most cohabiting couples have never really taken off their masks. They're still dating each other. The date may last a long time, but there's still no permanence to it. And so both partners try to keep their best foot forward at all times.

If they ever do marry, the masks finally come off. They can begin to relax, to be themselves. Of course, trouble soon follows, because they've already established patterns based on their masks. The Prince Charming she's been living with turns back into the frog he really is. The dazzling Cinderella he's been with, 24/7, goes back to the cinders.

The reality of marriage is hard enough to deal with, but it's worse when you've been playing house for a few years.

I suppose we really can't fault the logic that prevails in many young people's minds that the best way to test the waters of married life is to try them out—to live together and see if it's going to work. However, that's a little bit like learning to play basketball by playing badminton. The two are really unrelated. The cohabitation approach is destined for failure. There is a tremendous difference between "living in" and marriage. People who are merely living together are still thinking in terms of "mine" and "yours," whereas two people in a marriage relationship must be thinking in terms of "ours."

Now I'm not pointing the finger at young people who decide to live together on a trial basis, and I'm not judging them, because they've seen the mess that many of those in the older generation have made when it comes to marriage. But the remedy for the problems the older generation has experienced is not to live together without the benefit of marriage.

Someone once said that only fools say "never," but here I go anyway. If marriage is not the most important priority in your life, you are *never* going to have a real marriage, a marriage that includes commitment, that is full and satisfying emotionally, sexually, and spiritually. A live-in situation is a commitment, but it's a commitment *not to make a full commitment!* Women I have counseled who have lived with lovers all seem to share a common complaint: They feel cheated that their lovers didn't marry them. They feel that they lost their mates because they lived together instead of opting for a traditional marriage. They have come to realize too late that the live-in arrangement has very little to offer them.

In his book *Traits of a Happy Couple,* Dr. Larry Halter gives five specific reasons why marriages get into trouble, and I'd like to touch briefly on those.[1] They are:

41

1. The breakdown of pleasing behaviors
2. Skill deficits and negative pressure tactics
3. Negative communication behaviors
4. Low self-esteem
5. No time together

Incidentally, Dr. Halter's conclusions are based on ten years of research involving 130 "family scholars."

Let's take a look at these, one at a time.

## THE BREAKDOWN OF PLEASING BEHAVIORS

A complaint I hear constantly from wives is that their husbands just don't listen to them. The same man who used to hang on his sweetheart's every word when they were dating now tunes her out the minute she starts to speak. Why? Because he's no longer worried about pleasing her, about doing everything within his power to show her that he cares about her.

No doubt there were occasions when they were dating when she would bring up some subjects that weren't really of interest to him. But he wanted to please her, and because he was so interested in everything about her, he made every attempt to listen attentively. But now he just grunts and turns back to the newspaper.

Or perhaps the husband is an avid fan of professional sports. When he and his wife were dating, she seemed interested in learning about some of the nuances of the game. She might ask him what was meant by a play-action pass, or the infield fly rule, and really seemed to be interested while he explained it all to her. She didn't mind going to a football game once in a while, or sharing a bowl of popcorn while his favorite basketball team was on the tube.

But now that they're married, she has no time at all for sports. She thinks it's dumb to spend so much time watching a bunch of grown men run around bumping into each other and doesn't hesitate to let her husband know how she feels.

What has happened here? In both of these cases—the husband who won't listen and the wife who shows no interest in something that is important to her husband—there is no dedicated attempt to please the spouse.

Maybe you haven't thought about it for a while, but it's a good idea to ask yourself, "What can I do that would really please my mate?" Chances are that your mate doesn't need a four-karat diamond, a million dollars, or a cruise around the world. All he or she really needs is a demonstration from you that you really are anxious to please him or her. If you're married and things aren't going that well, perhaps you can think back to when you were dating and see some things you did differently.

And don't say, "Yeah, but *he* doesn't treat *me* the same either." We're not playing tit for tat here. That's a game that eventually escalates into an all-out war. We're talking about restoring a marriage to what it could and should be. And even though it may take some time and persistence on your part to make it happen, it is generally true that sooner or later you are going to get back what you give.

Give anger and you'll get anger back. But try to please your spouse, and he or she is going to be more apt to try to please you too.

## SKILL DEFICITS AND NEGATIVE PRESSURE TACTICS

What Dr. Halter means by this is that couples try to change each other by nagging, putting each other down, pouting, or using any number of other negative methods.

But you know, there's an old proverb that says you can catch more flies with honey than with vinegar. Sometimes there's a lot of truth in those old proverbs.

I read about a woman who had recently moved to a small town. She had to go into a local drugstore and was absolutely appalled by the way she was treated. The pharmacist, who was also the store's owner, was much too slow, she didn't like the attitude of the clerk, and there were several other problems that frankly ticked her off.

Later that afternoon, she began to complain to her next-door neighbor about the service she had received in the pharmacy.

The neighbor seemed to be concerned and said, "Listen . . . I know Tom, the pharmacist, really well. Maybe I should talk to him for you."

The woman said, "I wish you would!"

A few days later, she had cause to go into the little drugstore again, and this time everything was totally different. The pharmacist was pleasant and efficient, the clerk—who was his wife—was friendly and helpful, and it was a complete contrast to her first visit to the store.

When she got back home she called the neighbor and told her what had happened. "I guess you talked to him, just like you said you would."

"I sure did."

"And you really let him have it, huh—told him how unhappy I had been?"

There was a brief pause on the other end of the line. "Well . . . no . . . not exactly."

"Well, what did you tell him?"

"I told him you were absolutely delighted by the service he gave you. I told him that you loved his little store, and you planned to be a regular customer."

Well, I'm not sure if the story is true, but I know that the point it illustrates is true. Positive tactics work much better than negative tactics when it comes to changing behavior.

## NEGATIVE COMMUNICATION BEHAVIORS

Dr. Halter lists several "Communication Killers,"[2] and among these are:

- Negative Problem Description: A statement of the problem that is too long, too vague, or too emotional.
- Cross Complaining: Instead of listening to your mate's complaint, you immediately jump in with a complaint of your own, as in, "So I don't listen to you, huh? Well, *you* never want to take the time to talk about anything that's really important."
- Criticism: Always pointing out your mate's short-comings is not helpful, even if you think you are offering "constructive" criticism. And watch your tone of voice, because that often says just as much as or even more than your words do.
- Exaggeration: Sentences that use words like "always" or "never." "You *always* drag my mother into this." "You *never* take my feelings into consideration." You are not doing your marriage any good by overstating the case and making exaggerated generalizations.
- Negative Mind Reading: This is assuming that you know what is going on in your spouse's mind and accusing him or her of wrong motives. If you must assume, assume that your mate's motives are pure. Do your best to avoid statements that you could be sure of only if you could get inside your partner's mind—statements such as, "You're only doing this to make me feel bad."
- Overtalk: Refusing to give your partner "equal time" by monopolizing the conversation.
- Blaming: Always trying to assess blame and never being willing to share it.

45

- Problem Orientation: Continuing to describe the problem or focusing on past history instead of looking for positive solutions.
- Sidetracking: Using irrelevant sentences that reflect the inability to stick to the point during a problem-solving discussion. Or using sentences that jump from one problem to another instead of focusing on the problem under immediate discussion.

You can see how these negative communication behaviors could be harmful in a marriage. If you are falling into any of these patterns, do your best to stop yourself, apologize, and seek to approach things in a more positive way.

## Low Self-Esteem

You are probably as tired as I am of the endless self-esteem books on the market. It's getting so that you feel abnormal if you *don't* have poor self-esteem, but then I guess you can feel bad about being abnormal.

But don't let the self-esteem craze blind you to the simple truth of the matter: Healthy people have a healthy view of themselves. They're not the "king of the world" nor are they the "scum of the earth." They're gifted and growing, fallible but forgiven, humble but hopeful. Created, fallen, redeemed, empowered.

This healthy view of yourself is especially important in marriage, because it's raised to the power of two. You can help each other maintain a good balance in your self-understanding, or you can throw each other dangerously off balance.

I've seen a number of cases where a person with low self-esteem seemed to seek out a mate who reinforced that negative image. That may sound crazy, but let's face it—human beings are not always rational.

For example, I have counseled many women who went from being abused by their fathers to being abused by their husbands. They picked out husbands who treated them the way they had come to feel they deserved to be treated. They had married guys who were just like "dear old Dad," only Dad wasn't so dear. The person with low self-esteem may be overly submissive and compliant, and as we said earlier, marriage works best when it is understood to be a partnership between equals.

Another marital problem stemming from low self-esteem is that a person who feels bad about himself may be defensive and see innocent actions on the part of his spouse as put-downs, insults, and criticisms of himself as a person. He feels that he *deserves* to be put down, insulted, and criticized, and so he reads those things into innocent gestures, questions, and statements.

If your mate suffers from low self-esteem, the answer is to face the problem head-on and get him to deal with it. He may need to read a book or two on the subject. He may need professional counseling. But most of all, he needs a mate who will force him to face up to his problem in this area—someone who will expect him to stand on his feet and be an equal partner in the marriage relationship.

## No Time Together

Another reason why many marriages are in trouble is that couples don't spend time together. And this is something I don't understand at all, even though I've seen it many times.

The husband uses his weekends to go fishing or hunting with his buddies, he bowls in a couple of leagues during the week, and on the nights when he's not bowling he's likely to be working overtime. The wife, on the other hand, has a full-time job of her own, is involved in her club, and spends her weekends on shopping trips with "the girls." (Or maybe it's the wife who goes hunting and fishing on weekends and the husband who goes shopping with "the boys." There are seventeen marriages like this in the continental United States.)

Whenever I come across a marriage in which the couple doesn't spend time together, I always wonder why they got married in the first place. Presumably, they love each other. And if they love each other, why don't they want to spend time with each other? In some cases it's almost a matter of, "Well, we're married now. See you later."

I do not think that husbands and wives should spend all of their time together. There's no reason to suffocate your partner by demanding that he or she spend every available moment with you. There's nothing wrong with a husband spending a weekend in the mountains with the guys, or with a wife having an occasional night out with her friends. Taking small vacations from each other can be healthy in several ways.

But if your spouse is your life's top priority, then you are going to spend most of your free time with him or her.

Someone says, "Oh, but you don't understand. My schedule is so busy—I've got something going almost every night of the week. My wife will just have to understand that that's the way it is."

Let me say it again: If your spouse is your life's top priority—and certainly that's the way it ought to be—then you are going to spend most of your free time with him or her. After all, the way you spend your time shows what your priorities *really* are. And if your busy schedule doesn't allow you to have time to spend with your spouse, then it's time to rearrange that schedule.

I realize it can be difficult to find time for each other—especially if you both work, if you have children, and if you're involved in community or church activities. But a good marriage is more than worth any effort it takes.

I always suggest that married couples spend at least one night a week doing something alone together. It might be taking in a movie. It might be going for a walk in the park. It could be dinner in a nice restaurant. Whatever you do, it should be something that is mutually enjoyable, and you should have a strong commitment to it. If something comes up that cannot be avoided, reschedule your evening out to another night of the week—but don't cancel it altogether.

Those then, are Dr. Halter's reasons why many marriages are in trouble, and I would like to add one more of my own.

That is:

## LACK OF BASIC VALUES

I know a guy who has worked in a factory for nearly twenty-five years. Every night he comes home from work, flops down in his easy chair and watches TV, migrates to his computer room to play some computer solitaire, and lets the world roll by.

He may think life is just grand, but I think it's a distressing way to live—without passion, without interest in anything that's of lasting value. There are things in life that are worth believing in and worth fighting for.

It's not my intention to preach to you, or to tell you what to believe, but my personal feeling—which is backed by my years of experience as a psychologist—is that marriages that take into account the spiritual side of life are much better than those that don't. These are marriages in which the husband and wife both understand that there are eternal values and strive to live their lives in accordance with those values.

There is a deeper meaning to life. These deeper things need to be a part of your marriage if it is going to be all that it can and should be.

## Action, Not Words

In the next chapter I'm going to talk about birth order and how it impacts the marital relationship. But first, I want you to do a couple of things to strengthen your marriage relationship.

- Make a point of telling your spouse that you love and appreciate him or her, and if you have children, do it in front of them.
- Do something to show your appreciation for your partner. Send "I love you" balloons to his office, or send her flowers for "no reason except that I love you." If you can't afford balloons or flowers, then send a romantic greeting card—but do *something*.
- Make a date with your spouse to set aside at least one night a week for just the two of you.

# 3

## Whom Did You Marry?

I have this nasty habit I just can't shake. Wherever I go, whoever I'm with, I feel a compulsion to do it—even with complete strangers. My own family has learned to expect this behavior, and in a way they accept it, even if some of them roll their eyes. "There he goes again." Yes, I guess I've embarrassed them in front of waitresses, cab drivers, and airline attendants, but I just can't stop myself from this consuming fascination . . .

. . . with birth order.

That's right. I'm always asking people whether they're first born or last born, middle children or "lonely onlies." In fact, I often guess their birth order based on their appearance, occupation, or a few simple facts about them. About nine times out of ten, I'm right. I've dazzled stars like Katie Couric and T. Boone Pickens, seminar attendees, and an army of airline pilots by correctly guessing their place in their families.

It may seem like a parlor game, but it's actually based on solid psychology. Birth order determines a great deal about our personalities. There are exceptions, to be sure, but your status as first born, middle, only, or last born explains a lot about who you are. It also tells you a lot about your mate.

As you seek to understand your spouse—to anticipate needs, fulfill desires, and bring pleasure to your spouse—you need to know how he or she was raised. It makes a big difference whether your spouse was the leader of the pack or the baby of the family, and how that fits with your own birth order.

I hadn't been in private practice for very long when a woman called and told me she wanted to make an appointment for her son and daughter-in-law. I wondered for a moment why they weren't making the appointment themselves but went ahead and scheduled some time for them.

Well, when the couple came in I was shocked by their problem. It seemed that they had been married for seven months, and they had yet to consummate their relationship. They hadn't made love—not even once!

Tom and Johanna were both the babies of their families. What's more, they both had several years separating them from their older siblings. Because of this, they bore qualities of both last borns (which they were) and first borns (with a large gap, the order sort of starts over). As last borns, they were experts in taking from others and very poor at giving. But as first borns, they were perfectionists. They didn't want to do anything "wrong," even when it came to something as natural as expressing their love for each other in a physical way.

They were both waiting for the other person to take the first step when it came to sex. They were a little bit like two kids in the school yard who are about to fight. One kid says to the other, "Okay, you start it," and the other one says, "No . . . you." So they circle each other and circle each other some more, but nobody starts anything.

Well, Tom and Johanna never started anything. And I must admit that I couldn't get to first base with them. They simply were not able to make a commitment to each other, and after they had missed three scheduled appointments, I finally wrote them a letter referring them to someone else in town. I knew that I could not do them any good.

Two weeks later their names appeared in the newspaper as petitioning for divorce. I felt bad, but I wasn't surprised. You can't make someone do what he doesn't want to do.

Now Tom and Johanna both had the personality characteristics of first-born children, and when I think of two first-borns marrying each other, I envision two rams on a mountainside, butting heads. But as last borns, Tom and Johanna also had the habit of waiting for others to do things for them. Remember that it was Tom's mother who made the original appointment. I'm guessing the divorce was set in motion by some lawyer the mother knew.

Perhaps you have never taken the time to think about birth order, but where you and your spouse were born into your respective families definitely has a great deal to do with the way you relate to each other.

Birth order plays a significant part in your personality, and if you want proof, just look at the personalities of your brothers and sisters—or of your children.

If you had a brother or sister who was serious, intellectual, scholarly, an achiever or overachiever, chances are very good that the child was the first born. If, in the same household, there was a rough-and-tumble aggressive child, a social butterfly who always seemed to have a dozen friends hanging around, he was probably somewhere in the middle. And then there was the one who was forever showing off, who was less likely to be spanked or disciplined by his parents. The one who carried his nickname into adult life. That one, no doubt about it, was the baby.

## THE FIRST-BORN CHILD

Perhaps you are the oldest in your family. Or perhaps your husband or wife is the oldest in his or her family. If so, it's important that you understand some of the personality characteristics of such people. Only if you understand what makes a first born tick can you get the most out of a relationship with such a person, whether that person is your spouse, your child, your friend—or maybe even yourself.

If you're a parent, you undoubtedly remember the day your own first born came into the world. That was a special time, wasn't it? It was probably the most exciting day of your life. And most parents will admit that we place some of our unfulfilled dreams and expectations on that first-born child. He's going to be the person we always wanted to be—the one to bring glory and honor to the family name.

Yes, well. You can see the heady expectations that confront the first born the minute he sees the first glimmer of light from the outside world.

First borns are in a precarious position because they have so many pressures on them, but many of them handle the pressures beautifully and *do* go on to bring glory and honor to their families.

For instance, of the first twenty-three astronauts the United States sent into space, twenty-one were first borns.

The other two were onlies. There are many other vocations that also seem to draw the oldest child in disproportionate numbers. Accountants, engineers, computer programmers, architects, doctors, and attorneys tend to be oldest children. And that's no surprise, because the oldest child is not only an achiever—he is ordered, controlled, and very well organized. And I don't know about you, but I would hate to be treated by a doctor who wasn't organized, or defended in court by an attorney who wasn't completely up on the latest cases and rulings.

Since a first born's parents are new at the child-rearing business, they do tend to overreact to this child. Every hiccup is cause for alarm, and every new adventure is cause for rejoicing. Even a dirty diaper can send the mother and father of a newborn baby into a euphoric state. No wonder many first borns have an inflated view of their own importance to the world at large!

Another problem for the first born is that his parents tend to be inconsistent in their dealings with him. They try one thing, and if that doesn't work, they try something else. Such a child may become fearful and apprehensive because he doesn't really know where he stands.

But things aren't all bad for the first borns among us. They are also in an enviable position because they have their mothers and fathers to themselves for a time. Research tells us that first-born children tend to walk and talk sooner than their brothers and sisters, and a large part of this is certainly due to the attention they get early in life.

They are read to, played with, and encouraged to do things far more than their younger siblings—or at least that's the general rule. And it's easy to understand why. When that first-born child takes his first shaky steps, his mother and father act as if he's the first child who's ever been able to walk. It's sheer hysteria:

"Honey! Honey! Did you see Brewster? He just let go of the couch and took a step!"

"He did! Oh, my gosh, I can't believe it! Come on, Brewster . . . walk to Mommy! Walk to Mommy!"

But then by the time little Oscar takes his first steps, three children later, the scene goes like this.

"Honey, have you seen my gray socks? Oh, by the way, Oscar just let go of the coffee table and walked across the living room."

"Well, that's nice. Hmmm . . . I think they're in the hamper."

Perhaps I'm exaggerating just a tiny bit, but that's a pretty accurate depiction of the way parents react to their oldest children as opposed to the younger ones.

That's why first borns tend to be very much tuned into adult values and feel more comfortable dealing with adults. They are the ones who enjoy adult conversation and are offended when they are excluded from adult activities. They also tend to be dependent upon the family—meaning that they will uphold the family values and that approval of the family is important to them.

First borns are achievers, reliable, conscientious, apprehensive, and conservative. This means that the first born is likely to be a hard worker, a good provider, and someone who sees that all the needs of his family are met. He is also likely to be a perfectionist, a characteristic that is sometimes detrimental to him. Are you a first born, or are you married to one? What kinds of problems are you having in your marriage that could be directly attributed to this birth order?

Remember, first of all, that every birth-order position has a number of good characteristics. Unfortunately, each of those good characteristics can lead to trouble if it is overdone.

For example, the first-born child may tend to be competitive by nature. This is great when it comes to his career. It's what helps him to get ahead, to achieve a position of authority, and to provide well for his family. But, on the other hand, it can also cause him to view marriage as a competition rather than a partnership.

If you are married to a first born who seems to see everything as some sort of race, the best thing you can do is let him know that this isn't the way you see it, and you are not interested in competing with him. Because approval is so important to first borns, you can let your oldest-child wife or husband know that you appreciate her or his accomplishments, and that you admire the dedication to achieve. But you can also demonstrate through words and actions that you view marriage as a partnership, and that you want to work together instead of in competition with each other.

Meanwhile, you can also be willing to let your mate shine in front of others. Try not to feel slighted because he's getting some attention or feel embarrassed if he seems to view everything as a competition. It's in his first-born nature, and it is going to be difficult for him to change, even if he's trying hard to do so.

If you are a first born yourself, you may have to rein in your own competitive urges. If you realize that you've been guilty of trying to outperform your mate instead of working hand-in-hand with him, the first thing you can do is to tell him that you realize what you've been doing and that you are going to try to change things. Let him know that you've discovered that this urge to excel and achieve is part of your first-born makeup, but that it is not your intention to turn your marriage into a track meet. Apologize for any mistakes you've made in this area, and ask for your mate's understanding and help when you lapse into this sort of behavior.

Now let me acknowledge right here that the 100 percent, red-blooded first born probably read that word *apologize* and thought, "What???!!! Me, apologize! I can't do that!" Oh yes you can. It's hard for most of us to apologize. It's never easy to admit that we were wrong. But it can be especially hard for the perfectionistic, do-everything-right first born. But I sincerely believe that the words "I'm sorry" are among the most important in the English language, and next to "I love you" they are the most important your mate can hear from your lips.

Now I mentioned earlier that a marriage between two first borns is an especially difficult proposition—two rams butting heads. This is true not only because of their competitive natures, but because first borns tend to be people of tremendous organization. And two first borns may clash over how to organize. In other words, they may have specific routines and regimens for dealing with the world. The husband's system won't work for the wife, the wife's system won't work for the husband, and so both of them feel off-balance and angry.

I knew one couple, for example, who fought over how to approach almost everything in life, including how to water the lawn. She wanted to start the sprinkler in back of the house and gradually work around to the front. He wanted to start in the front and work around to the back. Yes, I know, that's not the sort of thing that should send a marriage to divorce court, but it was symptomatic of everything else in their marriage. And it was only with a great deal of effort and compromise that this couple learned how to live together in peace and harmony.

A key to overcoming these first-born tendencies is to understand that they exist and why they exist. Once you know why you relate to life as you do, or why your mate relates to life as he does, it's easier to get at the root of the problem. If you are a first born, the best thing you can do is to force yourself to let your mate take the lead once in a while. If you are married to a first born, the best thing you can do is to let your mate know that you are not interested in competing with him, and then to refuse to be drawn into any unnecessary battles.

Another strength of the first born is his tendency to do things right, but here again this can become a negative if he overdoes it. The most perfectionistic first born I've ever come across was a woman who not only ironed her sheets, but who went through the house with a tape measure every so often to make sure all of the furniture was where it was supposed to be. All of the chairs had to be precisely so far from the wall, from each other, etc.

There was a movie some years back called *The Accidental Tourist*. In it, one character was so compulsive that everything in her pantry was arranged in alphabetical order. Farfetched? No. A woman I knew did exactly that! Her life was so structured that she was making life miserable for her husband, her children, and even herself. What could she do?

It was only with the greatest of effort that we were able to work some intentional sloppiness into her life. I urged her, for instance, to go off and do some shopping one morning without making the beds. It doesn't sound like much, but it was almost more than she could bear.

She admitted to me that all the time she was shopping, she was thinking about those unmade beds. But at least she did it. It was a small victory, but it paved the way for other small victories that eventually brought about a healthy change in her lifestyle—and in her relationship with her husband and children.

One first born wrote to me after reading my *Birth Order Book*. "In my closet," he said, "dress shirts are on blue hangers, dark shirts on the left, lighter-colored shirts on the right; sport shirts are on brown hangers." Later he wrote about a crisis he faced when his housekeeper hung his dress shirts on *brown* hangers instead of *blue* ones. Horrors! How could he face the day?

Mercifully, he didn't fire that housekeeper. And he took a step in the right direction when he got rid of his brown hangers and started using only blue ones.

Another perfectionistic first born told me that her life changed for the better the first time she reached for a can of spaghetti sauce instead of spending hours making her usual homemade variety. There was something liberating in that one simple act that helped to set her free from a lifetime of slavery to perfection.

A moment ago I mentioned a scene from the movie *The Accidental Tourist,* and that brings to mind a scene from another popular movie of a few years back. In *Broadcast News,* someone sarcastically says to the perfectionist news producer, played by Holly Hunter, that it must be wonderful to always know that she's the smartest and best, that she can do things so much better than anyone else. The character totally misses the sarcasm of the comment and begins to sob, "Oh no! It's horrible."

Well, that's the prison the overly perfectionistic first born finds himself in. He is always having to prove that he can do it—whatever "it" may be—better than somebody else. He has to be the one who cannot be described without superlatives—the best, the smartest, the most artistic, the fastest, ad nauseam.

Researchers have detected a "cycle of perfectionism" that first borns all too often go through. It starts with the "all or nothing" mentality common to perfectionists—if it's not perfect, it's worthless. This leads them to take on too much, to "bite off more than they can chew." If they can't do *everything,* then *they* are worthless.

Panic sets in when perfectionists see the impossible tasks ahead of them. "How will I ever do all that?" That's the burden of perfectionism: setting a row of impossibly high hurdles in front of yourself, and knowing you'll never clear them all.

As a result, perfectionists get down on themselves. They focus on their failures. Even if they do something well, they know it could have been better. Sometimes the pressure gets to them and they bail out, leaving projects half-done, often with some excuse that preserves their perfectionist ideals—"I just didn't have enough time." But then they resolve to do better next time, to try harder, to achieve more. And the cycle continues.

If you know someone like that, do him or her a favor by helping him inject a little sloppiness and relaxation into his life. Every day this person has to defeat the perfection in his life, to learn to accept himself and others as they are.

## Action, Not Words

If you are part of a marriage that seems more like a competition than a partnership, you can:

- Take some time every day to hold each other and spend a few moments reflecting on some of the good things in your life together that you tend to take for granted: health, children, friends—whatever benefits are a part of your life.
- Force yourself—if you have to—to spend some time together at least once a week, just relaxing. Take this time to share your feelings and to talk about matters that are not achievement-oriented.
- Throw that tight schedule out the window and do something spontaneous. Inject a little sloppy spontaneity into your lives!

### ONLY CHILD

The only child tends to be the first born in triplicate. In other words, most of the characteristics of first borns apply to "lonely onlies" as well—only to a greater degree. They tend to impose very high standards on themselves—standards they carry over into marriage and parenthood—and tend to be superreliable, superconscientious, and so on.

For years it was assumed that only children were self-centered, spoiled, and lonely. Parents were urged to have at least two kids (if not the hard-to-attain average of 2.4) so they wouldn't deprive their child of siblings. But more recent research has debunked those ideas. Only children often have great initiative and solid self-esteem. And I should probably stop using the adjective *lonely*, because it isn't necessarily true. But it still rhymes.

Many only children have done extremely well in life. They're represented by such diverse successes as Dr. James Dobson of Focus on the Family; Steve Allen, the comedian who has also penned 10,000 songs; model and Princeton grad Brooke Shields; and TV anchor Ted Koppell—just to name a few.

## THE MIDDLE CHILD

To dramatize the plight of the middle child in a family, I usually ask the parents about the photo album. They'll laugh because they know where I'm going, and they also know I'm right. How many photos do you have of the oldest child? Oh, maybe just fifty or sixty thousand or so. Next question: How many photos do you have of the middle child (or children)? Hmmm . . . let's see . . . altogether there are . . . uh . . . fourteen. And nine or ten of those have the oldest child in them too.

Such is the difficult plight of the rather anonymous middle child. But it's not all bad.

For one thing, second-born children (and those who come afterward) have had someone who has plowed the roads of life for them. They have an instant playmate and, more importantly, they have a model. Now if the "model" first child is temperamental, throws temper tantrums, and refuses to do what Mommy and Daddy ask, then chances are good that the second born is going to go out of his way to be more pleasing to his parents. This is especially true if this second child is the same sex as the older child.

By the same token, if the first born is a scholar who is reading by the time he's three and never gets any grade below an A- in elementary school, we can expect the second child to seek notoriety in some way other than academically. Think of a tree sprouting and branching off in various directions; so it is with children in the family. And the kind of child you are is a strong indication of the kind of adult you will be.

Because most first borns tend to be perfectionistic over-achievers, most middle borns are oriented toward the social side of life. Due to their place in the middle, they make very good peacemakers and negotiators. Think of the two U.S. presidents in the last half-century who were known for their skill in foreign diplomacy. Most people would think of Richard Nixon and George Bush. Both were middle children.

Middle borns also tend to make friends easily, and they are loyal. If you are a middle born, or if you are married to one, I'm sure you'd be interested to know that middle borns as a whole are the most faithful marriage partners. They are less likely to "fool around," although I realize we are talking broad generalities here.

Middle children also tend to take life in stride and to let undue stress roll off their backs like water off a duck's back. Yet they are tenacious enough that when a problem comes along, they want to dig in and get it settled. They don't like troubled waters, and for that reason a marriage involving a middle child is often a very good marriage.

As one middle-child client told me, "Being a middle child of three wasn't easy, but as an adult I really believe I can cope with problems better because I got a lot of good training in give-and-take while I was growing up."

However, as with the first borns, there are some aspects of the middle child's personality that can cause problems.

For one thing, because the middle child is so good when it comes to compromise, he may be reluctant to tell you what he really thinks about some issue. On occasion he may say that he doesn't care much one way or another about something when he really has strong feelings about it. If you're married to a middle born, you may have to learn how to be a mind reader to ensure that you are not trampling on his feelings.

You may say, "Honey, do you feel like going to the ball game tonight?"

He says, "Whatever you want is fine with me."

"But really, don't you have a preference?"

"Oh no. I'm happy either way."

But he's really thinking, "Ball game? Oh, I'm so tired. I'd just like to stay home and watch TV."

So he goes along to the game and tries to mask his true feelings, only sooner or later his general grumpiness about the situation is going to show and cause some friction. If you are married to this sort of middle born, you need to stress to him the fact that you really do want to please him, and that means you honestly value his input. If you *are* this type of middle born, then you need to understand that your viewpoint is just as important as anyone else's, and then speak up so that those who love you won't have to play a little guessing game regarding what you really want.

Another area that can be a problem for the middle born is that he tends to find his value in what his peer group thinks of him. In other words, he is extremely susceptible to peer pressure, and even as an adult he may be doing some things to win the applause of the group—like spending money you really don't have on something you really don't need, just because "everybody else" has one.

Susan and John had been married for seventeen years when they called for a counseling appointment. They were both middle children whose own kids were entering their teenage years. They were looking down the road to the day they would be by themselves once again and wanted to ensure that they had a good, solid relationship when that day finally came around. They had a healthy relationship with occasional disagreements but wanted some help in making their marriage even better.

It's fairly typical of middle borns to want to negotiate a problem out of existence before that problem really even gets here.

I believe that Susan's and John's tendency to be mediators helped their marriage become a good, positive union of two people. They admitted to having some spats and disagreements, like most couples, but through the process of negotiation they were able to sit down and face things head-on. If their relationship needed anything it was a little fine tuning—certainly not a major overhaul.

## THE YOUNGEST CHILD

A fascinating book came out a few years ago from Frank Sulloway, a research scholar at the Massachusetts Institute of Technology. In *Born to Rebel: Birth Order Family Dynamics and Creative Lives,* Sulloway distinguishes between first borns and "later borns." Throughout history, he says, first borns have tended to uphold the status quo while later borns challenged it. He has gathered information on thousands of people who participated in scientific, social, and political revolutions over the centuries, finding that an overwhelming proportion of them were later borns.

It's brilliant research, but not surprising to me. Sulloway's "later born" group includes both middle children (known for creative solutions and dealmaking) and last borns (who tend to draw attention and do their own thing). It only makes sense that these two types of people would be "born to rebel."

We've just examined the traits of middle children. Now let's see how the last borns grow up.

The youngest child in the family tends to get away with murder. He's the type of person who is likely to go laughing his way merrily through life and right into the poorhouse or the divorce court. They are the Billy Crystals, Eddie Murphys, and Jim Carreys of the world. They are very funny people.

In other words, the last born is not the most responsible, dependable fellow in the world. He is likely to appear to be helpless, manipulative, charming, and very good at getting others to do things for him. Youngest children are special in that their births mark the end of the trail, so to speak. This is one of the reasons they are generally treated with "kid gloves" by their parents. They're always the youngest and smallest, so Mom and Dad are always coming to their aid, even if they need that aid about as much as Bill Gates needs another ten bucks. Another reason why some parents go easier on the last born is that they're just plain worn out from raising their other children.

The last born is always hearing from his siblings: "Mom and Dad never would have let *me* get away with that!" And most of the time it's true. The problem this creates in the life of the last born is that he is not likely to be very disciplined or achievement-oriented. As a rule he is not used to putting up with pain or discomfort; he is used to having things his way.

Generally speaking, though, last borns are not malicious or mean. There is a certain disarming quality in their self-centeredness, and they are likely to be fun-loving and happy-go-lucky people whom others enjoy having around. One reason for this is that the baby of the family gets used to being the center of attention. After all, he's got older siblings who look after him, ooh and ah over him when he's still an infant, and who say things like, "Oh, look . . . he's putting Daddy's hat on! Isn't he cute!"

I'll never forget hearing one man, the youngest in his family, confess that he never knew chicken noodle soup had chicken or noodles in it. He never had to make it, never even had to open a can. He just ate it! Last borns can seem ignorant of a lot of the street smarts their older siblings pick up (especially first borns), but they're comfortable in the spotlight from an early age. They don't mind being the center of attention. They can usually make up for any ignorance with charm.

The last borns are also in the enviable position of having older brothers and sisters to model.

If you're married to a last born, you're likely to find that your spouse is a fun, spontaneous, affectionate person. But he's going to need a gentle nudge every so often to keep him toeing the line and facing in the right direction. He's more than likely going to be a spontaneous sort of person who will think nothing of impulsively blowing several hundred dollars on a new "toy" or an unplanned getaway for the two of you. You may like that sort of thing, but it's probably going to be left up to you to occasionally say, "We just can't afford this right now."

Put two last borns together and well . . . all I can say is that I really don't think I'd want to see their credit card bills.

I suspect that the creator of the Nike catchphrase, "Just do it," was a youngest child. That is the prevailing attitude of last borns. They'll worry about consequences later. For now, they just want to go ahead and do it.

When I think of a marriage that involves the baby of the family I can't help but think of my own. As the youngest of three children I got away with far too many things in life. I really thought that God sent my wife special delivery to me to meet all my needs. After we returned home from our honeymoon we lived in a residence hall with 360 men on the University of Arizona campus. We were so naive at the time that we didn't realize that this was a demanding way to start the marriage; but we had very few problems adjusting to the new environment.

Things went amazingly smoothly. I used to come home at night, take off my clothes, and drop them wherever I happened to be standing at the time. Sande, who is a first born with a need to be neat and orderly, went around and picked up after me, and I thought we had an absolutely terrific relationship. It was just like the arrangement I had worked out with my mother for the first twenty-three years of my life.

It was only after hearing me talk to a parents' group on the subject of accountability training that Sande got the idea that her husband needed some training of his own. That was when things began to get progressively messier in our apartment. I didn't think a great deal about it until the day I came home and couldn't get the front door open. There was something on the floor—blocking it.

I pushed, and pushed some more, and finally got it open far enough that I could see the cause of the trouble. The floor was covered with a foot-deep pile of my clothes.

Poor Sande had decided drastic measures were called for. She had tried just to leave my dirty clothes where I left them, figuring that after a few days I'd get the message and pick them up. But I didn't, and I wouldn't. If that smelly pair of socks stayed in the corner for a week or two, that was perfectly fine with me.

She had finally become so exasperated by my lack of responding to her gentle hints that she had emptied every one of my clothes drawers and scattered their contents all over the apartment. I finally caught on—even though I was a slow learner—that Sande expected me to be a partner in this marriage.

I'm still not perfect in this regard, but I'm much neater than I used to be and positive proof that you *can* teach an old last born some new tricks. And looking back on that incident, I marvel that Sande was able to leave my dirty clothes on the floor the way she did, which was totally against her first-born nature. That illustrates that it is possible to modify your natural tendencies for the sake of your marriage.

If you are married to a last born, it's a good idea to take a look at his family. What is his relationship with his mother and father? You can probably get a pretty good idea about some of the work that you might have to do. Unfortunately, too many men grow up believing that a wife is a personal maid. They don't know how to do a thing for themselves—and this is especially true of last-born males. You might need to introduce him to a few of your special friends: Mr. Washing Machine, Mr. Oven, Mr. Vacuum Cleaner, Mr. Dishwasher. . . . Not that you want to turn the tables on him and make *him* do all the work—but you need to get him to see that marriage is a fifty-fifty proposition. Besides, you need to know that he will be able to survive for a few days when you go off to help your sister with her new baby!

Of course, it's not only the last-born male who seems to be allergic to housework. Almost all of us men could use a little retraining in this area. If the marriage is the traditional one in which the husband works and the wife takes care of the house, then obviously, the lion's share of the housework should be done by the wife—although the husband needs to pitch in. But in the situation where both marriage partners are holding down full-time jobs, then the housework should be shared on a fairly equal basis.

Now as far as the men are concerned, if your wife was a special princess in the family who was always the center of attention, all I can tell you is that you've got your work cut out for you! The truth is that you will need to be especially attentive to her or she may become disillusioned with marriage.

## Action, Not Words

Whom did you marry? A good exercise for you and your loved one is to spend some time talking about your respective families. How much do you know about your mate's family? Do you know how your husband or wife (or boyfriend or girlfriend) feels about his or her brothers, sisters, and parents? As you talk, try to determine what roles were acted out within the family unit. Who was the black sheep? Who was the mediator? Who was the manipulator? Don't be accusing or pry beyond what makes your mate comfortable, but use the discussion as a fun opportunity to get to know each other better, and thus to improve your relationship.

Why are we taking this minicourse in psychology? Because the little boy or girl you once were, you still are. The little boy your husband once was, he still is. The little girl your wife once was, she still is. The old proverb is true, "the child is father of the man," and to understand the man or the woman you have to understand the child within.

Once you discover that you've married the pampered princess in the family or the instant wonder of the world, the baby, the first thing you have to come to grips with is that it's difficult to change the leopard's spots. But you can change your own behavior in such a way that your mate's behavior is no longer a menace to you. In other words, if your husband is a first-born perfectionist, you can allow him to have extremely high expectations for himself, even as you let him know that you do not expect to be held accountable for fulfilling his unrealistic expectations.

If you married a man who has been pampered, whose mother did everything for him, a good, honest communication session is in order, along the lines, "I'm not your mother. I don't want to be your mother. I want to be your wife. I expect you to treat me like your wife, and that means that you treat me like your partner."

No, he won't want to hear you talk like that, but he *needs* to hear you talk like that, and that is what's really important. And husband, if your wife is "too tired" every night for romance, then perhaps you should take a look around and see what you're doing that contributes to her fatigue. Leaving your clothes lying around for her to clean up, failing to help out with dinner preparation or with the cleaning up after dinner—these are some of the things you may be doing that reflect your unhealthy attitude toward her, and these things are easy enough to change. Modify your behavior in some of these areas, and you are likely to see her behavior begin to change too. Not only will she not be so tired, she will also be appreciative of your attitude, and she will be in a more loving mood as a result.

When you change your behavior, you *allow* your mate to change his or her behavior because he or she *wants* to change. Always keep in mind that you can't paddle another person's canoe for him. But you can make sure that your own paddling is strong and steady and on course.

Do that, and pretty soon the other person will be paddling right alongside you.

## EXCEPTIONS TO THE RULE

If you haven't seen yourself in any of the descriptions of the various birth orders, then it's highly probable that your situation comes under the heading of "exceptions." There are a number of variables that affect the development of personality characteristics.

Some variables may be:

- Physical/emotional differences
- Sex of children
- Years between the births of children
- A miscarriage or death of a child
- Parents' interaction with individual children
- Parental criticism
- Blended families

### PHYSICAL/EMOTIONAL DIFFERENCES

If your older brother or sister is handicapped in some way—whether physically or mentally—you may be a middle born but likely developed along the lines of a first born. Or suppose your older sister's handicap was that she was always small for her age, with the result that even though you were younger, you were bigger and looked older. Then you are likely to be, for all intents and purposes, the first born in the family. And, in a case like this, the older sister is likely to become discouraged and defeated over what she sees as her inability to measure up. The handicap doesn't have to be terribly severe to cause some changing and rearranging in the family's pecking order.

## SEX OF CHILDREN

If you are a girl who has an older brother—or vice versa—it is likely that you have the characteristics of a first born rather than a middle born, but that depends to some degree on the outlook of the family in general. If the family has similar expectations for boys and girls, then the second-born child of the opposite sex will more than likely develop the characteristics of a middle born. But if the family has a different set of expectations for boys and girls—that is, if the girl doesn't feel that she has to compete against her brother because he's more interested in things that pertain only to boys—then both children are likely to have first-born tendencies.

In a family of three older girls and one boy, you don't have to be a psychologist to figure out that the first-born girl and the last-born boy will be very special in the family. If any of the children tend to be the "black sheep" it would be the third-born girl. Having a "king" born right after her could impair her self-esteem and take away her sense of specialness.

In a family where there are five boys and one girl—even if that girl is somewhere in the middle, she is still likely to develop along the lines of a last born. That's because she is so "special," being the only female, and she's likely to be pampered and spoiled throughout her young life.

And, of course, the only boy who has several sisters is likely to be an even stronger example of a last born because he is going to be spoiled not only by his parents but by his sisters as well. I believe that older sisters in general—because they are more interested in babies than boys are—treat their little brothers much better than older brothers treat their little sisters. (No, I don't have any studies to back me up on this, but experience tells me this is true. Especially experience with regard to my wonderful older sister, Sally!)

### YEARS BETWEEN THE BIRTHS OF CHILDREN

If there is a gap of five or six years or more between the births of children, you are essentially going to wind up with two first borns. So it is quite possible, particularly in a large family, to have two or more children with first-born tendencies. If you had four children, and there were five years between each of the births, then it's even possible that you could wind up with four first borns in a family. The reason for this is that the passing of years reduces the need to compete. If one child is in the fifth grade, and his brother is in the fourth, the younger child is likely to hear from his teachers, "I just hope you do as well in this class as your brother did." But if the child in the fourth grade has a brother who's in the ninth or tenth grade, that sort of pressure is not likely to be there, and he won't have to go off in another direction to find his niche.

### A MISCARRIAGE OR DEATH OF A CHILD

This tragic variable has a great impact on the entire family, but the biggest impression is made in the life of the child who is born following the miscarriage, or who is next in age after the child who died. What happens in such an instance is that this child becomes "special" to the parents. He is likely to be pampered and overprotected because the parents don't want to "lose" him too. He will thus have the characteristics of a last born in a very big way.

### PARENTS' INTERACTION WITH INDIVIDUAL CHILDREN

In a typical family, various roles will be assumed by different children: There might be the scholarly first born, the comedic second child, the athletic third child, the artistic or musical or black-sheep fourth child. We can usually predict the role each person will assume in that family, and once a role is taken it is rarely challenged or changed. And parents are as likely as anyone else to relate to their children within the framework of the roles those children have taken for themselves.

You will find families where all the children are athletic, scholarly, or musical, and there is no rivalry. What has happened here is that the parents have done a masterful job of parenting and of dealing with their children in a noncompetitive way. This is a family where everyone feels free to participate, where all the children's strengths are encouraged and appreciated, and where there is no stress related to winning or losing.

### PARENTAL CRITICISM

A parent's critical eye can turn an overachieving first born into a procrastinator. You know the kind of parent I'm talking about, the one who can spot a flaw a mile away and won't hesitate to mention it. First borns of these parents can lose their initiative, becoming the kind of children you have to push at every turn.

In such cases, the first borns often retreat to a safer position and act more like middle borns. A second- or third-born child, shielded from the parent's criticism by the older siblings, can emerge as a "functional first born" in the family.

### BLENDED FAMILIES

The family models we saw on *The Brady Bunch* and *Eight Is Enough* are now becoming commonplace in real life. Divorce and remarriage are putting families together in all sorts of combinations. I call it "the birth-order blender." The patterns of one family are suddenly merged with those of another, and you can imagine the chaos. Mom's first born may be a middle child in the new arrangement. The baby of Dad's family may get lost in the middle of the new muddle. A child who used to get all the attention may suddenly be ignored—and may start acting out. Another child who used to take the lead may suddenly be vying for pre-eminence with one or two step-siblings.

This creates strange combinations of characteristics, as you might guess. A lot depends on how early the blending occurred. If a child enters a stepfamily around age three or four, he or she will quickly adapt to the new birth order. But if we're dealing with teenagers, the die is already cast. Whatever birth-order roles children grew up with in the first six or seven years of life will set the birth-order patterns for the rest of their lives.

Again, everything we have discussed in this chapter has been for the purpose of helping you to understand how you and your mate developed a series of personality traits. These personality traits are quite logical, and isn't it good to know that your mate doesn't really do all those things just because he wants to irritate you?

## Action, Not Words

Take some time to diagram your own family, the family your mate grew up in, and the family where you are now the parents. Beside the name of each person use an adjective to describe him or her. Then see what conclusions you can draw from the diagrams. Can you see reasons why you and your mate developed the way you have? Can you see how you are contributing to your children's developing along certain lines? Remember, the little boy or girl you once were, you basically still are.

Your diagram might look something like this:

## Husband's Family

Festus (husband) 41      Perfectionist, reliable, accountant
Harold (brother) 39      Easy-going, artistic
Buford (brother) 38      Charming, salesman
Beatrice (sister) 35      Manipulative, demanding

## Wife's Family

Sally (sister) 45      Bookkeeper, temperamental
Samantha (sister) 43      Independent, competitive, career-oriented
Sissy (wife) 39      Easygoing, helpless, homemaker

## Our Family (Dad, Festus; Mom, Sissy)

Phineus 13      Scholarly, apprehensive
Hurkimer 12      Rebellious, sloppy, athletic
Princess 9      Independent, cute, demanding
Moose 3      Spoiled (rotten), strong-willed, precocious

Can you guess why Festus and Sissy were drawn together in marriage?

# 4

## Making the Pieces Fit

I'm cohosting a TV program called *RealFAMILIES*, and I love the concept. We tape in front of an audience and try to solve real-life problems that people face. The fact is, lots of "experts" churn out advice that sounds good in theory but falls apart when you try to take it home. This program is a way of keeping me honest, of making sure that what I say really makes a difference with real families.

That's my hope and prayer for this book too, that you would learn from it and apply it in your real-life situation. For instance, this birth-order material is fascinating stuff, but it won't do you much good unless you use it to understand yourself and others in your family a bit better.

In the previous chapter we talked about how your birth order has affected your development as a person and how it has probably affected your marriage. Now we're going to move on to talk about "lifestyle analysis"—a process by which we go back and put together the pieces to the puzzle of your childhood in order to help you understand how you got to where you are today. In other words, we're going to take a look at the society that surrounded you as a child—your mother, father, siblings, and possibly other close relatives such as grandparents—those who are generally in your immediate family.

As we do so, we will talk about the development of several personality types that can get in the way of successful, fulfilling, happy marriages. These are:

- Attention-getter
- Controller
- Martyr
- Pleaser
- Carrot-seeker
- Cop-out artist
- Revenger

One of the things that most psychologists, psychiatrists, and mental health workers agree on is that our personalities form in the first few years of our lives, and that they are generally pretty well developed by the time we are six or seven years of age. Like many other things in life, personality traits and characteristics are learned by trial and error. This personality development results in how we behave—because we behave in a way that works for us, serves a purpose in our lives, and gets us to a desired goal. Over time, a way of behaving is continuously reinforced and is eventually ingrained into the daily life to such an extent that it becomes a lifestyle.

The lifestyle you established for yourself in childhood is resistant to change. Unless you undergo psychotherapy or are faced with some kind of traumatic experience or make a concerted effort to change your ways, you can be pretty sure that you will still be displaying well into your golden years the behavior you displayed as a youngster.

Now, let's take a quick look at the lifestyles of the personality types that we mentioned a moment ago.

## THE ATTENTION-GETTER

There is no chance at all that the "attention-getter" is an endangered species. The fact is that there are millions of them. One of them may be your husband or wife. You may be one yourself.

The attention-getter can be found in two birth positions in the family in disproportionate numbers. He is usually a first born, or else he is a baby. The first born is more likely to seek attention in a positive way, while the baby will go about it in a negative fashion. The first child tends to become an attention-getter because of the love and attention he receives from his parents—the overwhelming excitement that greets his arrival into the world. This attention-getting nature is even more pronounced when he is also the first grandchild in the family. With so much adult attention paid to every movement of his early life, it doesn't take long for him to decide that he is the center of the universe.

For example, take what happens when a first-born one-year-old boy, sitting in his high chair, decides that he doesn't like his strained rutabagas and throws his spoon. Instead of being angry, Dad picks up the spoon and says to his wife, "Did you see how far this kid threw that thing? What an arm! Why, I'll bet he's going to be another Brett Favre."

The child, seeing the adult reaction, will watch his daddy put the spoon back on the high chair, and then he'll throw the spoon again, this time giggling as he does so. Dad, still impressed with the "strong arm" of his boy, continues to smile and laugh about it, essentially praising the child.

About the thirteenth time little Junior throws the spoon, Dad starts to get irritated. But his initial reaction has already caused the baby to understand that he can get attention and play enjoyable games with the adult by displaying this behavior.

Let a middle born try this sort of trick, and he's likely to get a lecture about being "naughty." Dad and Mom have both seen this kind of thing before, and they're not as interested in seeing it again.

Children learn early in life that they can do things that command their parents' attention. And attention can quickly become its own reward—even if the attention received is of the negative variety. If the only time a child gets the attention he craves from his parents is when he misbehaves, then you can be certain that he will misbehave more and more frequently. If we pay more attention to the child at the times when he is doing things that are outside the family guidelines, then we are really reinforcing the unwanted behavior.

I mentioned earlier that the first born is more likely to seek attention in a *constructive* way, whereas the last born may seek it in a *destructive* way.

We've already talked about the fact that the first born tends to walk and talk more quickly than his siblings, due largely to the fact that his parents work with him more. When he goes off to school, he tends to do very well, again, largely because of the influence of his mom and dad. He's ready for school and gets attention there, just as he does at home, by doing the right things. He learns how to read quickly. He is good with his numbers. He seeks out the attention that can come from being a "good citizen."

The destructive attention-getter, on the other hand, can get attention by always keeping an adult busy with him, by showing off, or by doing whatever else he can think of that will cause others to sit up and take notice.

He's the type who is likely to do something like taking a *Playboy* magazine to school to share with the other third graders, or taking out his scissors and cutting the ponytail off the girl who sits in front of him, or shaving the cat. The person who seeks attention in a negative sense will try just about anything once. In fact, I remember a little boy who used to eat pencils.

"Sherman, why are you eating your pencil?"

"I don't know."

"You don't know? Do you *like* pencils?"

He shrugs. "I guess so."

Sherman got what he wanted, which was plenty of attention. Word got all over the school. I mean, he was almost famous, as in, "Hey . . . are you that kid who eats pencils?" Sure, they looked at him a little funny at times, but at least they were looking at him, and that's what he wanted.

Only, I wonder what old Sherman is eating these days. Does he get attention at the office by chowing down on a desk calendar or a floppy disk? What in the world does he pack in his lunch?

So you can see that a certain amount of attention-getting behavior in and of itself is not a bad thing. It can spur a child on to heights of achievement. But if he goes about it in the wrong way, there's no telling how or where he may wind up. And, of course, an inordinate need for the attention of others is never healthy. When I think of grown-up attention-getters I think of a young couple I worked with many years ago—Joel and Suzi.

As a child, Suzi was the princess in her family. Not only was she the youngest child in her family, she was also the only girl. This apple of Daddy's eye was precocious, demanding, and very good at getting others to notice her. She used her charm, cuteness, and temper to demand attention.

Joel had grown up as the "man" of the house because his father had died when he was just nine. Joel had always been reliable, conscientious, and perfection-oriented. He was convinced that he knew what was best for everyone, including Suzi.

Joel was a bicycling enthusiast who like to go on "little" biking trips of, say, forty or fifty miles. He approached this area of his life the way he approached everything else—full throttle. He wanted to go faster. He wanted to go farther. He wanted to accomplish and achieve.

He just *knew* that his wife would love these trips too, so he invested several hundred dollars in a racing bike for her. On her behalf, I'll have to say that Suzi gave it a pretty good try before she decided that this just wasn't for her. She simply couldn't keep up with her husband, and she didn't find it particularly enjoyable chasing him down some country road and watching the distance between them grow greater and greater.

She decided that she had had enough of this particular sport, so for the next several weekends Joel left her at home while he rode off on his own. And Suzi became angrier and angrier. She wanted the attention that her husband was giving to that "stupid" bike.

One Sunday afternoon, Joel came home exhausted after a day of bicycling and immediately flopped down in front of the TV. That was the last straw for Suzi, who decided to voice her anger in a most definite way. Now Joel's other pride in life, besides that bike, was his prize bed of tulips. It was about forty feet long and four feet wide, with beautiful flowers in an array of colors. But that was before Suzi took the trimming shears to it. By the time she got through, there wasn't a flower left. Nothing but stems looking like a bunch of oversized toothpicks pointing toward the sky.

Yes, that act got Suzi some attention. It wasn't particularly *good* attention, but it was attention nonetheless. That's when they came to see me.

I made a great deal of headway with this couple because they were both able to see the driving forces in their lives—Suzi's need for attention and Joel's need to achieve—and to work on modifying their behavior. It took compromise and commitment on both their parts to make sure they met the other person's needs. Joel soon learned that every time he put his wife in the position where she was the center of attention, she purred like a kitten. And Suzi learned to give Joel credit for his achievements and that he occasionally had to have some time for himself. Joel, meanwhile, agreed to budget his time more equally—to do some things that Suzi liked to do. They also agreed on some set hours when Joel could take off and do his bicycling—and there were even some occasions when they actually did go biking together—but gently, side-by-side, instead of in racelike fashion.

## THE CONTROLLER

The controlling lifestyle is probably the most difficult to deal with, especially within a marriage. The controller tends to play his cards very close to his chest, only rarely giving his partner a glimpse of his real self.

There are basically two types of controllers: One controls because he enjoys pulling all the strings and being in charge of every situation; the other controls for defensive purposes—because he's afraid that someone else may take him down a path he doesn't want to follow. Basically, the controller is afraid. He is afraid that he will die, or afraid that he will lose his mind, or that others will betray him. He'd much prefer to stay locked in that protective shell, even though it keeps out the people who love him the most.

Fred was a controller who expressed his need to be in charge through intellectualizing, through being perfect, and through being hung up on neatness as a virtue in life. He was an accountant, a profession where many of his perfectionistic tendencies were useful. I'm sure you've heard of accountants who are referred to as "bean counters," and that's the way I always think of Fred. He was there with his stack of beans, counting each one over and over and making sure none of them got spilled or lost.

Linda complained that every time she went to cuddle up to or talk to her husband, he found something for his busy hands to become engaged in—such as washing the car, mowing the lawn, tending to the garden, or whatever else might be handy. It almost seemed to her as if he had a definite plan to avoid contact with her, except on the nights when he wanted sex. That's when he pursued her in a very methodical, clinical manner, without any overt consideration of or affection for his wife.

As you can imagine, Linda didn't react very well to what she saw as her husband's desire for sexual gratification. Because there was no affection, no love talk, no anything, except when he suddenly wanted to do the wild thing, she felt angry and used. For this reason, she didn't enjoy sex with him at all.

After several weeks of therapy with Linda, I got her to see that there was no use trying to make Fred into something he wasn't. All her pleading, coaxing, and reminding hadn't worked in their thirteen years of marriage, and it wasn't going to work now. I finally convinced her to begin to act in a totally different manner than before.

As she began to back off and give up trying to remake him, Fred realized that something was changing in their relationship. He saw that Linda was no longer under his control, and he was threatened by the fact that she was no longer chasing after him for "cuddling" purposes.

When she stopped chasing him and began to be independent of him he finally began to seek her out, asking simple questions like, "What's wrong? Do we need to talk about something?"

It was a pleasure to watch their marriage begin to come together, but it took determination, hard work, and commitment on Linda's part to stop playing her husband's game. And, of course, it also took a great deal of effort on Fred's part to change.

He finally admitted to me that he had always been afraid that if he told his wife who he really was, how guilt-ridden and inadequate he felt on the inside, she would reject him. He felt that it was the man's role to be the strong one, and he thought that to share his feelings was to display weakness.

They both told me that the highlight of their thirteen-year marriage was the night they finally wept in each other's arms. It is still easy for Fred to go back to the learned behavior of shutting people out. He has to consciously think about it and internally commit himself to being open with others.

This is what I refer to as "calling an audible at the line of scrimmage." What happens in football is that the offensive unit will go into a huddle and decide what play they're going to run. But occasionally, when the team lines up to begin the play, the quarterback will notice that the defensive unit has anticipated his play selection.

In other words, the defense is lined up in such a way that they are certain to stop the play he's selected. That's when he calls an audible—a number sequence that lets his teammates know to go to a different play.

Fred knows that his tendency is to be closed and controlled, to shut his wife out when she comes to him looking for a little affection. But he can call an audible and refuse to give in to his feelings. When his wife wants to talk to him about something serious, he may not feel like it, but he can say, "She needs to talk to me right now—it will help her if I share what's on my mind—and so I'm going to do it, regardless of how I feel."

Remember that you never have to go along with your feelings. There's always plenty of time to call an audible at the line of scrimmage.

Fred remembered that he had been very shy as a child, and I wasn't surprised, because shyness is one factor that can be used to control the behavior of others.

I remember working with a five-year-old girl who was sitting in the chair, talking in a sweet, gentle, and nearly imperceptible voice. I kept leaning over trying to get closer to her so I could understand what she was saying—and then it hit me. That little girl had me in the palm of her hand. I could almost hear the wheels turning in her head and wondered if she was thinking, "In another minute or two, I'll get the crazy psychologist to fall off his chair and onto the floor, flat on his face!"

When I stopped playing the game with her, it was amazing how loud her voice became.

You see, recognizing the controller isn't always easy. He may be the last person you would suspect of being interested in controlling others. But when he approaches you from a position of shyness, he is saying, "I want to make you pay attention to me. I want to control the situation because I'm special."

Controllers may use temper, tears, shyness, and intellectualizing to keep people at their distance. They tend to operate on the power principle that says, "I only count in life when I control."

The very best thing you can do if you are married to a controller is to refuse to give in to his controlling behavior.

## The Martyr

Okay, I guess I have to tell you all about the martyr now. But it's sure difficult for me to write this. All I do is write, write, write—in order to help you out. My fingers are tired from all this typing, and I'm getting a headache from all this thinking, and my eyes are getting blurry. And then I wonder if you'll even read it. But I'm doing it all for the sake of your marriage.

There . . . do you feel guilty enough? The martyr, you see, is very good at making people feel guilty and/or uncomfortable. Martyrs are difficult to deal with because they have the need to do themselves harm and they are always putting themselves in unenviable positions. They are perfectly capable of giving, but they haven't the slightest idea how to take. And for any relationship to be healthy, there needs to be a fair amount of both giving and taking.

A martyr is likely to be married to an alcoholic. Essentially, that's because an alcoholic needs a martyr to use and abuse, and martyrs have the deplorable need to be walked on.

The martyr generally develops the feeling early in life that he's not worth loving. He tends to have a poor relationship with his opposite sex parent, and then goes out and chooses a life partner who will reinforce his negative interpretation of himself.

I worked with a martyr, Janet, who had recently married for the second time. Janet was agoraphobic, meaning that she was afraid of being in open spaces. I realized that she was a martyr when she explained that she was having terrible panic attacks in supermarkets. She would get to the point where she had to run from the store because she felt that her air supply was being cut off and she was about to faint.

Although she hadn't told me very much about her marriage, I said, "Janet, I'll bet you anything that your husband is an alcoholic."

She looked surprised and said, "Well, he is. But how did *you* know?"

I said, "I didn't know, but I guessed, because you've just told me that you really are a martyr. You had to run out of the store for fear that someone else would see you faint."

What I was hearing from her was that she didn't think she was worth the attention she would get if she fainted in the store. Martyrs just don't think they're worthy of anything.

If you came upon an accident in which the martyr's leg had been cut off, he'd probably say, "Oh, don't worry about me. I'm sure I can get along without that leg. Why don't you see about that poor guy over there. I think he's got a broken fingernail. Oh yes, sure . . . the pain is excruciating . . . but you go on. I'll be fine."

I worked with a couple named Johnny and Alice, who had a martyr living with them. She was Alice's mom, and she was driving them crazy. She was getting up there in years and was doing a good job of making her daughter and son-in-law feel guilty if they went anywhere and left her home alone. They were going out of their way to be ever-sensitive to her needs, with the result that their own marital relationship was suffering.

It was only when they began to make the commitment to take care of their own relationship first that Mom's martyr-like behavior began to decrease.

When I think of a martyr, I think of the woman who is married to an abusive husband but refuses to leave him. Or the wife who enables her alcoholic husband to continue in his destructive lifestyle by covering up for him, making excuses for him, and saying, "If only I love him enough, everything will work out okay."

I admire a wife who wants to help her sick husband. There's something to be said for the woman who loves her man and stands by him, even when his behavior is completely unlovable. But only up to a point. If the abusive husband refuses to get professional help so he can deal with his hostility, then the wife has no choice but to leave him. If the alcoholic husband will not take steps to overcome his addiction, the wife ought to get out of the marriage.

It is true that most martyrs are women who are married to extremely controlling men.

The martyr who leaves the situation that is causing her to be degraded is often taking the first positive step that she has ever taken in her life. This is a reaffirmation of the fact that she is worth loving. It's very difficult for people who have been stepped on and squashed over a long period of time to get to the point where they gain some notion of self-esteem or respect, but it can be done.

I sometimes suggest to the martyrs I counsel that they look at themselves in the mirror and say, "I *am* worthy of love. I *am* worthy of respect. I *am* worthy of being treated well."

I also strongly suggest to the martyr that she do something nice for herself (or occasionally, himself). Her assignment before the next session may be to buy herself a new outfit, or to take one entire evening to do something that she'd really like to do—just relaxing with a good book, soaking in a bubble bath, attending a concert, or doing anything else that she would find particularly pleasurable.

It's not easy for the martyr to engage in something that is terribly self-indulgent—but again, major changes in lifestyle can best be brought about one small step at a time.

## THE PLEASER

Now let me introduce you to the martyr's sister. Her name is Patty Pleaser.

91

The basic difference between the martyr and the pleaser is that the pleaser wants everybody everywhere to approve of everything she does.

In the film *Forrest Gump,* Tom Hanks played a mentally challenged man who was the ultimate pleaser. Spouting his simple philosophy ("Life is like a box of chocolates"), he did his best to help everyone. His people-pleasing put him in a number of interesting historical situations— earning a medal for saving a buddy in Vietnam, joining an antiwar rally, reporting a break-in at the Watergate Hotel. He just wanted to be a nice guy. He just wanted everyone to be happy.

Pleasers are like that. They tend to go with the flow, afraid to express their honest opinions. In many cases, they're attention-getters who learned early in life that the best way to win approval is not to make waves. Go along to get along.

The pleaser can make it in life for a while. But then one day he begins to think, "What about me? What about *my* needs? When is someone going to meet *my* needs?"

And then you have people saying, "I don't understand it. How could she have run off to Mexico and left her husband and children like that? It just doesn't seem like her."

No, it doesn't always come to that, but that's one reason why anyone who is married to a pleaser needs to seek to open the doors of communication by asking questions such as, "What do you want in this situation? Come on . . . tell me what *you'd* really like."

All too often, the husband is more than happy to take advantage of his pleaser wife's lifestyle instead of doing his best to help her overcome it. He's content to watch her rush around with a plastic smile on her face, doing everything she can for him, and never noticing that those eyes behind the smile are becoming angrier and angrier . . . until it's too late.

In my counseling, I've learned to ask certain questions to determine whether a person is a pleaser. I say, "If you are in a restaurant and are served a meal that is not to your liking, what do you do? Do you send it back to the kitchen, or do you go ahead and eat it, even if it's not even what you ordered?" The pleaser will usually go ahead and eat it because he doesn't want to make waves, and then he'll leave a big tip to boot!

My wife, Sande, has some of the tendencies of a pleaser, and those came into play one night when we were having dinner in a very nice restaurant. I don't know what it is about going to a fancy restaurant, but when we do we always order things we wouldn't order in other restaurants. So I had Long Island duckling and Sande ordered salmon. When the salmon arrived at the table, it looked as if it still had a fighting chance of getting upstream to spawn. Sande commented that it wasn't quite done but she began eating around the more fully cooked edges.

I thought to myself, "No way am I going to pay for that!" So I called the waiter over and told him that the lady's salmon was not done and asked him to please return it to the kitchen. He was most apologetic and quickly took her plate away. Moments later the maître d' came to our table and expressed his sincere apologies. Two minutes later the headwaiter came over, relaying the chef's apologies and bringing the news that the chef was preparing a little something for our dessert, compliments of the house, as his way of showing how sorry he was for not having the dinner prepared correctly.

Within a few minutes, the salmon was back on the table, done to perfection. And when we were finished, the waiter brought us baked Alaska flambé, covered with a pure marshmallow sauce, drenched with fresh strawberries!

Since then, whenever I go to that restaurant, I always complain about the way my meal is cooked, in hopes of getting another terrific dessert. (I'm only kidding, of course, but I'd do almost anything for baked Alaska.)

You see, the pleaser does not want to do anything that might cause waves—that might cause other people to be angry with him. And there are times in life when you have to run the risk of making other people angry.

The problem for the pleaser is that there are people who are always ready to take advantage of his or her "agreeable" attitude. The pleaser wife and mother may be in a car pool with four other women, all of whom are supposed to drive the kids to school one day a week. And instead, she finds herself driving at least two, and sometimes as many as three days a week. That's because whenever one of the other women wants a break, she knows that the pleaser won't say no to the question, "Can you please drive for me today?"

The pleaser husband and father may refuse to stand up in defense of his family because he doesn't want to make waves. For example, his son Tommy may come home from a neighborhood baseball game and say that Billy Johnson hit the ball through Mrs. Smith's window. Only Billy lied and said Tommy did it, and now Mrs. Smith expects Tommy to pay. The pleaser is likely to say, "Well, don't worry about it. I'll pay for the window," instead of standing up for his son and telling the truth to Billy's father and Mrs. Smith. He doesn't want to cause waves, to create any hard feelings, but he's only paving the way for more problems for himself and his son.

Pleaser parents have a hard time disciplining their children because they want their kids to love them. "But if I ground her for the weekend, she might get mad at me!"

You can see some of the problems caused by the pleaser lifestyle. But what can you do to overcome it? Basically, there are three things:

1. If you are married to a pleaser, you can stand up for your pleaser mate at every opportunity, similar to the way

I did in the restaurant with Sande. I knew she didn't want to eat that half-cooked salmon, but it wasn't within her pleaser nature to complain about it. Even as you urge your mate to do a better job of telling you how he or she feels, you also need to do a little mind reading so that you can know, "My wife [or husband] really isn't happy about this, so I'm going to act."

2. You can also urge your pleaser mate to begin to speak up in his own behalf. You can show him through your own actions that sticking up for yourself doesn't have to be done in an obnoxious or overly rude way—and that it can and does bring benefits to your life.

3. If you are a pleaser, you can practice saying no. The next time someone asks you to do something you don't want to do, form your lips into that little round shape and just say "no." Practice saying "no" as often as you can, or expressing your honest opinion whenever you are given the opportunity. It will be hard to say "no" the first few times you try it. You may find yourself getting dizzy and your palms starting to sweat. But it will become easier, and before long you'll be standing up for yourself with only a modest amount of effort.

## THE CARROT-SEEKER

Due to our traditional upbringing of reward and punishment, many of us have grown up looking for a reward in everything we do in life. The carrot-seeker is one of these people—he simply goes around looking for a carrot at every turn. When he doesn't receive praise or reinforcement for every little achievement, he is deeply offended and hurt.

Very similar to the pleaser lifestyle, the carrot-seeker says, "I only count in life when other people notice what

I do and reward me for such behavior." Well, there are certain situations in life where the carrot-seeker can do very well. But that lifestyle generally becomes unfulfilling.

If a person has to receive a "thank-you" for everything he does, or expects some mention of approval, that person is a carrot-seeker. Eventually he must realize that he does things for others only to serve himself.

Don't think I'm saying that there's anything wrong with liking to be recognized. There isn't. And if you've done a particularly good job of something or other, then you certainly want people to notice.

A woman who spends four hours in the kitchen preparing a beautiful dinner for her family is going to be hurt if her husband and kids gobble down her dinner and then get up and leave the table without telling her how great it was.

A husband who spends a month of evenings in his workshop building a new set of cabinets for his wife may not be doing it just to get her praise and thanks—but he's certainly going to feel slighted if he *doesn't* get some appreciation and recognition.

But the carrot-seeker is a bit different. This is the person who volunteers for every single committee in the club and church for the simple motivation that he wants to be praised and recognized for all his hard work. The carrot-seeker husband and wife may try to outdo each other, but only because each is interested in getting the praises of the other.

For example, I counseled a young couple where the husband was always outdoing the wife when it came to housework. (Now there's a switch.) The problem was that he wouldn't let up. If everything else was caught up, he'd wash the windows or tackle the bathroom tile with a toothbrush. Now his wife was no slouch when it came to keeping up with things. And she'd sometimes say, "Come on, honey . . . let's go out for some coffee. I'll take care of that tomorrow."

His response was invariably, "Oh no, I'll do it now. I don't want you to have to worry about it."

It was only in therapy that he came to see that his total motivation was winning praise from his wife. He wanted her to tell her friends, "My husband's the greatest. You won't believe all the work he does for me!" He wanted her to be praising and thanking him twenty-four hours a day, but instead he was driving her crazy and making her resentful because she felt that he was trying to show her up.

Once he recognized what was prompting his behavior, he made a conscious effort to change and their marriage was saved. I often give the carrot-seeker the same assignment I give to the martyr. I tell him to do something for himself each week—whether it's joining a health club, taking a class at the local community college, joining a bowling league—anything that is outside the home, away from the children, and just for his personal satisfaction. The reward is that he is doing things that he feels to be worthwhile and not just that other people are going to be thanking him for. There are many good results that come from treating yourself in an okay fashion. The carrot-seeker has to learn that he doesn't need the approval and praise of everyone else—only his own feelings of self-worth and self-esteem.

## THE COP-OUT ARTIST

The person who has the cop-out lifestyle is generally either an oldest child or a youngest child. If he is the oldest, chances are that his parents had very high expectations for him. If he is the youngest, chances are good that the children above him were very successful, which had a defeating effect upon him. Cop-outs tend to be inadequate people—primarily because that's the way they see themselves.

Rarely do you see these people complete any kind of task. It's even abnormal to see them start tasks as they begin to grow older. Their mission seems to be to prove to others that they can't do anything efficiently or correctly. If something is going to be done in this person's life, it's going to be done through or by another person.

To help the cop-out artist, people who are close to him must withdraw from the scene, refusing to do anything for him that he can or should do for himself. In addition, the cop-out artist is likely to need good professional help.

The problem for this person is that he is so afraid that he will fail, even if he gives an honest effort, that he refuses to give an honest effort. He thinks it's better not to try at all. Oh, he *thinks* he's trying. But he isn't, really, and he can wreak havoc in his own life as well as in the life of anyone who really cares about him.

## THE REVENGER

One of the reasons I am pessimistic about rehabilitation programs for hard-core criminals and drug addicts is that they have been firmly entrenched in the revengeful lifestyle. That is a lifestyle in which the person believes life has treated him unfairly and he has a right to strike back in any way he can.

The revengeful lifestyle takes some time to develop, but it may be ingrained into a child's personality by the time he is eight or nine years old. From this time on, any hurt or punishment this person suffers only reinforces in his mind that life has been unfair to him and escalates his desire for revenge. It is the revengeful lifestyle that often manifests itself in senseless violence—and I would go so far as to say that the revengeful lifestyle is to blame for most of the violent crime in the world.

It's not very often that you see people in marital therapy who are into revengeful behavior. They're generally not the sort of people to admit that they need help. But Marion, who was thirty-three, was one of those I tried to help, even though it was her husband and not Marion who came to me. Marion had grown up in a home where her father had abused her and her mother before he deserted the family when she was only six.

Marion wasn't given much of a head start in life, but she nevertheless managed to become a good student and even went on to graduate school, where she received a master's degree in her chosen field. She wanted very much to have children of her own, but was unable, so she and her husband, Roger, finally settled on adopting a little boy.

Roger told me that one day he came home from work at the normal time and found the home in disarray and their three-year-old son, Jimmy, covered with bruises. He told me that Marion had always had a violent temper, and that he had thought sometimes she disciplined the child too harshly, but this was his first realization that she had become physically abusive.

Marion's revengeful lifestyle was manifesting itself in a most dangerous and ugly way. When things went wrong, she often overreacted to the point where she just wanted to harm the child. In this particular case, the son had to be taken from the home.

I wish this story had a happy ending, but it doesn't. Marion refused any kind of help. The only positive thing that came out of professional help was that Roger and Jimmy were able to get away from Marion, who seemed determined to vent her frustration and anger in a violent manner. Jimmy had to go through a series of counseling sessions so that we could allay his fears and frustrations. We had to get him to see that his situation had not been a normal one, and that little boys should not expect to be hurt by their mommies in this fashion.

Roger and Marion finally went their separate ways. Roger's leaving and subsequent divorce was really an act of love toward himself and his son, of whom he was awarded custody. Roger was saying, in essence, that he didn't deserve to be treated that way and neither did the little boy they had adopted. My guess is that Marion will continue to look for someone who needs to be used and abused and will probably remarry someday when she finds someone with those specific needs.

I would like to think that she will change, but I realize that the revengeful lifestyle is so deeply ingrained in her personality that change is extremely unlikely.

Another revengeful person I got to know was Gerald, a millionaire who owned property all over the world. He was a nationally known expert in his field, a man who was greatly respected by his peers. He had everything a man could want, including a beautiful, charming, and competent wife. And yet he was a very angry man. He had a violent temper and a booming voice to go along with it— and he often attacked his wife, Melody, verbally.

There were many times when she was so shaken by one of his outbursts in public that she ran from the room in tears. She made contact with me due to the fact that she was so uptight and nervous around her husband. She was beginning to develop gastrointestinal problems and migraine headaches. That uptight feeling was consuming her energy and keeping her from being productive.

When I talked with Gerald I found out what had made him that way. When I asked him to describe his earliest memories of life, he couldn't go back any further than the time he was sixteen years old, which was most unusual.

At age sixteen, Gerald remembered hearing a gunshot. When he ran into the next room to see what was going on, he saw his father holding a gun to his head. Gerald's father had killed his mother and then proceeded to take his own life in front of his son. That same day, the boy's sister killed herself. Gerald pulled down the steel curtain on his life and memory at that time. He was unable to go back and remember anything before that age until therapy helped to unlock his childhood for him.

In his mind, Gerald had a right to be angry and bitter—who wouldn't feel that way after suffering through something like that?—and he developed a revengeful lifestyle.

As a young man striving to make it on his own, Gerald had developed a tremendous amount of independence. He closed others out of his life, feeling that he would have to make it on his own, since he was the lone survivor of his family. And when he married Melody and they began to work together side by side in business, he would sometimes blow her away with his vicious explosions.

When I asked what precipitated these outbursts, neither one of them was able to give an answer. All Gerald could say was that there was something inside of him that would just snap and he would blow up. I asked Melody to write down the sentences that they spoke to each other just before an explosion, and we came to the conclusion that the key word that would set him off was *why*. Whenever she asked *why,* he felt that she was challenging his authority and/or wisdom and she would have an explosion on her hands.

I was able to help Gerald and Melody in their marriage simply by eliminating the *why*s from Melody's vocabulary. We were able to cut down the outbursts by 75 percent in the first two weeks. What's more, in therapy Gerald felt for the first time that he had "permission" to talk about his feelings—especially his anger and his need to exact revenge.

As he began to open up, the relationship between Gerald and Melody began to become more intimate. Even though he had always tried to repel anyone who tried to get close to him, he still had an urgent need to talk about his feelings, thoughts, and fears. But since his tragic family background was not known to any of his acquaintances, and since all those who knew him felt they had to go around walking on eggshells, no one had ever taken the time to really get to know him. They were business acquaintances and colleagues, but nobody had ever wanted to get close enough to be his friend.

The marriage between Gerald and Melody finally made it when we got them to the point where they could sit and talk about anything. With much work and understanding on both their parts, we finally got the relationship on stable ground. Without logically looking at the way our childhood determines the way we behave as adults, we never could have gotten Gerald and Melody to the place where they are today.

The important thing to remember about many lifestyles is that they are founded on falsehood. You don't really have to control or dominate or get others' attention in order to count for something.

It is important for us to be able to see that all of our experiences in early life are perceptions. Our feelings about our parents and siblings and our experiences come together to give us a biased perception of ourselves. This biased, predictable behavior pattern is acted out in the framework of our lifestyle. But a negative, destructive lifestyle does not have to be followed for the rest of your life. It may take a tremendous amount of effort to change it—but it *can* be changed.

# Action, Not Words

Why not try to get to know yourself and your mate better by understanding each other's lifestyle? Play armchair psychologist for just a moment. Take turns asking each other the following questions:

1. How would you describe your mother or father? (Give seven or eight adjectives that would describe personality, makeup, or temperament.)
2. How would you describe each of the siblings in your family?
3. How would you describe yourself as a kid—specifically as an elementary school-age child?
4. List ten recollections about life going as far back as you can remember.

When each of you completes the exercise, review your answers. For Question 1, the parent who had the most influence on you as a child is most likely to be the parent you described first. This is not to say that you got along best with that parent. In fact, that parent may have been absent from the home for most of your growing-up years but was still the most influential in your life, even if his influence was brought about by his absence and lack of involvement. If, in describing your parents, you use superlatives or adjectives preceded by "very"—such as very smart, very pretty, etc.—this is often an indication that you value that trait in your own life.

In Question 2, as you describe your siblings, you should begin to look for patterns or roles that are assumed by each of the children in your family. Diagram your family in similar fashion to the way you did in the earlier chapter on birth order. Begin to make some intelligent guesses about how you see yourself, how your mate sees himself or herself, and get a feel for each other's lifestyle.

As you review Question 3, keep in mind that it is generally true that the description you give yourself as a child is the same way you would see yourself as an adult. The little boy or girl you once were, you probably still are.

Question 4 might seem a bit too heavy for you to do, but if you'll take the time to do it I think you'll find it to be enlightening. Your earliest memory—that is, the furthest you can go back in time—is symbolic of the way you look at life or your lifestyle. If your first memory is negative, that might mean that you tend to see things in a negative or pessimistic way. If all of your recollections are negative, then it's fairly safe to assume that you have a negative outlook on life. If all the recollections were situations where you were the center of attention—where people were bringing you presents at Christmas and birthdays, and so on— then we can safely assume that your lifestyle is centered around attention-getting. If some of your early recollections centered around your breaking rules and regulations and being punished for those infractions, then we might make the guess that you are controlling. You are good now at keeping the rules and are not very flexible.

You can see how you can make some intelligent deductions about yourself and your mate by looking at the pattern of early recollections.

# 5

## One Plus One Equals One

Dad was just getting settled into his easy chair with the newspaper when he felt a small hand tapping at his knee.

He lowered the paper to see his five-year-old son, Bobby, looking up at him with an urgent expression on his face.

"Daddy," the boy asked, "where did I come from?"

Dad's face started to redden, and his palms began to perspire—but there was no avoiding the question.

"Daddy," the question came again, "where did I come from?"

With a deep sigh, Dad set the paper down, invited his little boy onto his lap, and launched into a ten-minute discourse on "the birds and the bees."

Bobby listened politely until his father had finally finished. "So that's the way it is, Son. Do you have any questions?"

"Yeah," said the boy. "I want to know where I came from. Susie Thompson just told me that she came from Albany, New York."

That father had just been involved in a classic case of miscommunication. If he had understood that his child's question was really "Where was I born?" he could have saved himself a great deal of talking and embarrassment—at least for the time being.

Well, miscommunication is a major problem between husbands and wives, and I couldn't write a book about relationships between the sexes without spending some time talking about communication. Even though "communication" is an overused word today, good communication is still one of the single most important factors in a marriage. If your marriage is typical, it's safe to say that you spend fewer than five minutes a day in real communication.

I recently saw a newspaper comic strip in which a couple is sitting in a marriage counselor's office. The counselor had given this husband and wife the homework assignment of being more communicative during the week.

The wife, complaining that her husband hadn't done what he was supposed to do, says that he's said just three things to her all week: "Where's my dinner?" "Where's the remote control?" and "What's that smell?"

The husband shoots back that his wife has said only two things to him, and they were, "You're sitting on it," and "Your socks."

The counselor looks at the husband and asks, "And which one of those answers had to do with 'Where's my dinner?'"

Of course, the noncommunicating, battling husband and wife have been fodder for cartoonists and comedians for centuries. But in real life, it isn't so funny. In fact, it can be hellish to be locked into a marriage where there is very little in the way of communication, of open and honest exchange of feelings and thoughts between partners.

I find that men and women are basically afraid to communicate, to tell each other who they are, to express their innermost thoughts, needs, and feelings. For our purposes, let's assume that when I use the word *communication* I mean "a sharing of yourself verbally and nonverbally in such a way as to enable someone else to understand what you've said and how you feel." Communication involves not only the sharing of words, but just as importantly, the skills of listening and understanding.

Not too long ago, a full-page advertisement in the *Wall Street Journal* caught my eye. A Fortune 500 company devoted an entire page (which had to cost a tremendous amount of money) to the art of listening, telling the readers that all their employees—from secretaries to corporate executives—go through listening seminars. When big business learns that it pays to listen, we ought to take note. Because the bottom line for business, I am sure, is the increased productivity as a result of good listening habits. If a Fortune 500 company is willing to invest so much time and effort in the process of listening, for the sake of corporate success, then certainly you and I ought to be willing to invest our individual time and energy in it for the sake of our marriages.

Communication between a husband and wife usually goes something like this. Husband walks in the door at night and announces, "Hello! I'm home. How was your day?"

"Fine," she says, knowing that he's not really interested in hearing about the hassle she had with the Brownie troop she leads. "And how was yours?"

"Okay." (Well, the truth is that there were some big problems at work, but he's spent the day talking about them with his coworkers, and he doesn't feel like plowing that same old ground right now.) "What's for dinner?"

"Chicken."

"Great."

Now, what was really said in this conversation? Nothing more than, "I don't really want to talk about anything. I'm not really interested in sharing the details of my life with you, and I'm not interested in having you share the details of your life with me."

As a counselor, I have seen many good marriages fade, wither, and die as a result of a lack of communication.

I have also talked to many men and women who have become involved in extramarital affairs, and I guarantee you that the number-one reason for affairs is lack of communication between husbands and wives.

A woman has things on her mind that she needs to share with someone, but when she tries to talk to her husband, he lets her know in some way that he couldn't care less. He may pick up the newspaper and begin reading when she's trying to talk to him, or he may turn his attention to the game on TV. When his wife stops talking he turns to her and says, "Go ahead, I'm listening," but she knows he isn't, and she's hurt and angry. If she's trying to talk to him in bed, he may start snoring right in the middle of it.

But then there's this guy at work. He's just a friend—that's all. But he's willing to take the time to listen. He seems to understand and care—certainly more than her husband does. And in time, she begins to think that there is something more than friendship here—and the result is a full-blown affair.

An affair doesn't come about because the wife is tempted by some Tom Cruise look-alike—or because the husband is lured into infidelity by a painted, padded seductress.

I once talked to a man who was married to a gorgeous woman and yet was having an affair with a woman who could only be described as "plain." Why was it happening? Again, because the "plain" woman gave him something he needed—something his wife denied him—she was genuinely interested in what was on his mind and in his heart.

Do you care about your husband? Do you love your wife? Then take the time to strengthen your communication skills, especially the art of listening.

## They Don't Know How

Perhaps the most prevalent reason for the lack of communication between husbands and wives is that they just don't know how to communicate. The husband who walks in the door with "Hi, honey! I'm home. What's for dinner? Where's the mail?" is showing an appalling lack of skill at communication. Most of the time these words communicate the message that "I am not really interested in carrying on any type of feedback. Nor am I interested in expressing how I feel."

Jack, forty-three, and Dottie, forty-one, had been married for twenty-one years and were raising five children. Being a blue-collar family, they had to scrape for every nickel they could get; but basically, things went well throughout most of their apparently typical marriage. However, when I first saw Dottie she had just been released from a residential psychiatric treatment center. In her own words, she had suffered "a nervous breakdown." She told me that she had always tried to be a good mother and wife—the sort of person other people wanted her to be. She was always doing things for others, while she sacrificed and went without.

Finally, the time came when she was totally spent—mentally, physically, emotionally—and she collapsed like a building being imploded.

As Dottie related her situation to me, I had the hunch that the sexual relationship between her and her husband was not good. I couldn't have been more right. Dottie admitted that in twenty-one years of marriage, she had never once experienced an orgasm, nor any sort of sexual fulfillment. This aspect of her life, like all other aspects, was a duty—something she did for her husband.

As I pressed Dottie for some background information on her breakdown, she told me that her washing machine had gone on the fritz about six weeks previously. Jack assured her that he would fix it "this weekend," and then "next weekend," and so on, but the time never came. You can imagine how important a washing machine is to a family with five children. When Jack continued to put off fixing the washing machine, things began to close in on Dottie to the point where she chose to "go under."

Notice that I said *chose* to go under. Mental illness is not "caught" but is often a learned behavior that *serves a purpose* in one's life, either consciously or subconsciously. In this case, Dottie's choosing to go under was her way of making her husband pay attention to her. She decided to cop out of life for a three-week stay in the treatment center, which cost her husband more than five thousand dollars. He would have been ahead if he'd just called the Maytag repairman.

There was still another factor involved. Although Jack couldn't find the time or money to fix some of the broken appliances around the home, he had scraped together enough to buy a secondhand pickup truck. That incident contributed the final blow for his wife.

Jack finally woke up to the fact that he had been negligent as a husband. Dottie's absence from the home made him understand what a tremendous contribution she made to the entire family. He had to take some time off work and become a homemaker while his wife was undergoing treatment. And yes, you can bet that one of his first acts was to get the washing machine fixed.

The real Jack surfaced when he began to demonstrate to Dottie, both before and after her release from the treatment center, how much he really did care for her. Not only did he begin to show more consideration of her needs and feelings by helping with the domestic chores, but he also contracted with me—and more importantly with himself—that each day he was going to set aside the time so that the two of them could spend some quiet moments sharing with each other. As soon as Dottie came home from the treatment center, he began to take her on walks, where they would stroll arm-in-arm for a couple of miles, sharing their innermost thoughts and feelings and deepening their relationship. This was something they had never done before, and to Dottie it was like a breath of life, bringing renewed purpose into her heart and her marriage.

Prior to this, I had asked Dottie if she and Jack had ever gone away for a weekend together—just the two of them—and she said that they hadn't. When I asked why not she said it was because they couldn't afford it. And yet Jack was able to buy that pickup, which he didn't really need, and they had a big television set and some other major appliances. Now I'm not suggesting that they should have done without the TV or any of the other "creature comforts" they had, but it seems to me that most people are able to afford the things that are really important to them. In other words, if something is a priority in my life, I can probably come up with a way to afford it.

Too many couples seem to have the idea that going away for a weekend is a waste of money, or a luxury, but it isn't. If you want your marriage to be all that it can be, you will invest in the relationship, and that includes as many romantic weekend getaways as possible.

Now remember that Dottie had told me that her sex life was totally unsatisfactory. So during an individual counseling session, I suggested that she should become *involved* in her sex life with her husband, rather than just being a recipient of his advances toward her. The first part of my suggestion had to do with Dottie inviting her husband out to dinner at a swanky local hotel.

She looked at me as if I had lost my mind. "Oh, no, Dr. Leman . . . we couldn't do that. If we get out to McDonald's every couple of months, it's a big deal."

But I successfully convinced her that instead of a $5,500 stay in a psychiatric treatment center, she would come out ahead by investing in the relationship. She decided to become a part of the therapy in a very action-oriented manner.

So Dottie made reservations for dinner *and* a room (the second part of my suggestion) and even placed fresh flowers in the room. After a very enjoyable dinner together she asked her husband if he would like to go for a walk. As they walked along the lagoon-like area, Dottie steered him past the reserved room. Suddenly she pulled out the key, plunged it into the keyhole, and to hear her tell it, pulled her husband into the room in one sweeping motion—like some Amazon woman. Yes, this was going to be *the night,* no two ways about it.

Dottie told me that she had written a love note in lipstick on the mirror, although she never did tell me what that note said. Remember, though, this was a woman who had so much trouble communicating her feelings to her husband.

When I saw Jack a couple of days later, the first words out of his mouth were, "Doc, I don't know what you did, but whatever you did it was beautiful."

Jack initially failed to see that I didn't do much of anything. Dottie's action had been encouraged by his efforts to demonstrate his love, concern, and affection for her. His attitude toward her made her feel like trying once again. And as for Dottie, she told me later that during that night in the hotel she had experienced her first orgasm in twenty-one years of marriage.

What happened was that Jack had come to understand that Dottie was worth loving in the truest sense of the word. He would no longer take her for granted and would make their marriage his top priority. He would do everything possible to see to it that the lines of communication were always open. As a result, Dottie and Jack now have a relationship that exemplifies "One Plus One Equals One," not only physically but also emotionally. I couldn't help but think of them as frolicking teenagers when I saw them in the office the next time. They couldn't keep their hands off each other!

I was almost embarrassed.

But I wasn't really, because it was fantastic to see this rekindled love in two people who really had always loved each other, but who needed to learn how to communicate.

## WE ARE AFRAID

A second reason for not communicating in marriage, besides the fact that we don't know how to talk to each other, is that many husbands and wives are afraid of sharing their real selves with their mates. They think that if they tell their spouses how they really feel about certain issues, their mates won't understand or will even reject them.

This is especially a problem for women who have taken on the lifestyle of a pleaser. They never want to be in disagreement with anyone, so they go through life trying to say, do, and be everything their husbands (or parents, or friends, etc.) want them to say, do, and be.

The attitude of being afraid to show who we really are is found in both sexes, but even though it is not limited to women, it is more prevalent among them. I believe this is due in large part to the fact that our society still teaches girls that it is "unladylike" to be opinionated, or at least to speak up when they are. A young man who knows what he thinks and isn't afraid of expressing himself is a "go-getter," "ambitious," and "has a lot on the ball." A young woman who does the same thing is often referred to by a derogatory term that rhymes with witch.

Why? Because sexism, as is the case with racism, takes a long time to die out.

I remember one woman who was afraid to tell her husband who she was because she just knew that he wouldn't want her anymore. Her name was Rita, and her husband was a fairly successful businessman who was actively involved in politics. (Although he himself was not interested in running for office.) The two of them were forever in the spotlight—photos in the paper, hosting a glamorous cocktail party, dining with some senator or congressman. And Rita hated every minute of it.

Rita wasn't the least bit interested in politics and wasn't even sure, in fact, that she agreed with her husband's position on at least half a dozen issues that were important to him. And she would have much preferred a quiet evening at home to another elegant dinner party in the town's best restaurant.

Another thing that was bothering Rita was that she felt her husband was always interested in showing her off, and she resented that. He would often surprise her with a new dress, usually just prior to some big wingding, but she felt that his tastes were either too ostentatious or too slinky. She also resented the fact that he seemed intent on doing her clothes shopping for her. Now Rita was an attractive woman who undoubtedly got some second glances in those "slinky" dresses her husband picked out for her, but she was embarrassed by the fact that he was trying to "show off" through her.

She tried not to wear those dresses, but he was so insistent and so proud, and she just couldn't let him know how she really felt. Besides, he *was* generous.

114

On one of her birthdays, he even presented her with a little red sports car convertible. Of course, she had really wanted a new Mr. Coffee machine to go under the cabinet in her kitchen. She figured that was typical, because giving her the sports car was another way he could show off and show her off.

It took a tremendous amount of prodding for Rita to get to the point where she could even begin to tell her husband how she felt. But because she knew the resentment and bitterness she was hiding inside were about to choke her to death, not to mention her marriage, she finally decided that she would have to tell the truth.

The only advice from me was that she should do it as firmly, but as gently, as possible. The resentment that had been building up inside of her was due, more than anything else, to her own inability to express herself. It was not fair to blame her husband for that, even if he was "guilty" of the other transgressions.

Rita picked a late-night dinner at a romantic restaurant to talk to her husband. She was afraid that she might back out if she didn't force herself into moving forward, so she told her husband beforehand that she needed to talk to him about something.

When the time came for her to say what was on her mind, the words wouldn't come at first. But then, as she began to express her innermost feelings, the entire torrent came rushing forth, and she told him exactly how she felt about everything.

I can't say that her husband's feelings weren't hurt. They were, and at first he reacted in an angry and defensive way. But when Rita reached out, took his hand, and told him that she loved him dearly but just *had* to tell him how she felt, that helped to calm him down and get him to begin to see things from her point of view.

She had done such a good job of acting all these years that he thought she *loved* being in the spotlight, and in fact, the main reason his feelings had been hurt is that she had waited so long to tell him how she really felt. Yes, he admitted he liked to show her off, but after all, she was beautiful and he was proud of her. He hadn't meant to put her on display. His actions had only been meant to say, "Hey, everybody, this is my wonderful wife and I love her."

He even admitted that he often felt unworthy of her and gave her all those fancy gifts as a means of making up for some lack that he perceived to be within himself. Rita felt, correctly, that this was the beginning of a whole new era of openness and honesty between them.

It wasn't easy for them to work out all the details of what life was going to be like for them from now on. He did not want to give up his involvement in politics, and there were many dinners and parties to which they were already committed. But he promised that he would cut back as much as possible, and that he would be more attentive to her needs and desires.

Now this story had a happy ending, but it might not have worked out that way. Rita's husband might have said, "What? You're not interested in politics? Then I'll find me a woman who is!"

But if that had been his reaction, then Rita would have been better off without him. I know that sounds flippant. But my point is that if someone really loves you, he is not going to try to make you over into his image. He is going to want to know what's on your mind and in your heart and cherish you because you have dared to share your deepest thoughts with him.

I remember a song the late Joe Tex sang, "Skinny Legs and All." The gist of the message was that if you don't want somebody because of some defect you perceive to be in him, just turn him loose and you'll be amazed at how quickly somebody else comes along to grab him. Do you think your husband wouldn't want you if he knew what you were really like? Are you afraid that no woman could care for you if she could look into your soul? Don't be ridiculous.

All human beings have weaknesses, fears, hurts, angers, and things deep down in their souls that they are embarrassed about or even ashamed of. This is the common state of humankind and does not mark you as a bad or inferior person.

## Action, Not Words

On a sheet of paper, draw a horizontal line about an inch from the top and a vertical line down the middle. In the left-hand column, above the horizontal line, write the words "real self" and on the right-hand side write the words "ideal self." Take a couple of minutes to write down a description of your "real self," the self you know you really are. Now devote a couple of minutes to describing the "ideal self," which is what you would like everyone else to think of you. What self does your mate know? Does he know the real self? If he or she doesn't know the real self, you are one of the many thousands of people who are afraid to open up and share because you fear rejection. Think how special it would be to have your mate know and love the real you without any qualifications whatsoever. Then work toward the process of letting your mate get to know the real you.

### Too Much Trouble

A third reason why couples don't take the time to communicate with each other is that they think it's too much trouble. Sometimes this comes about because a person has tried to share something of himself, only to find that the other person didn't really seem to care or responded with a hurtful remark.

When this happened, the person who was hurt decided, "Well, I'll never share *my* feelings again."

This kind of hurt may be pushed beneath the surface of a person's life, but it will never be buried so deeply that it won't cause some emotional and psychological problems. Very few people are able to continue to tuck away hurts without having those hurts begin to surface in some ugly ways.

Think of your emotional self as a teakettle on a stove, with the steam being your emotions and feelings. If you don't have the opportunity to let out your emotions and feelings in a constant and free-flowing manner, then sooner or later you get to the point where you blow your top. And a top-blowing experience can be destructive to any relationship, including a marriage.

Lucy had been divorced for the first time when she was nineteen, the second time at twenty-three, and the third time at twenty-eight. Her first husband was a rather shiftless, unfaithful, and irresponsible young man. He had joined the Navy and left her home—high, dry, and pregnant.

Only four months after her divorce was final she married Al. Then she found out that he had a problem with drugs, which eventually cost him his job. He wasn't faithful to her either.

Then she found Rowdy Raymond, who had all the charm of her first two husbands, as well as a violent streak.

To find out why Lucy was so good at picking men who could best be described as losers, I did a lifestyle analysis. I took the time to have her describe herself, her parents, her siblings, and her early recollections of childhood. Then we went step by step through every relationship she had ever had with men.

It was in all these descriptions and recollections of life that we found the reasons for Lucy's behavior. She was reinforcing her lifestyle, which was that she was not worth loving. I figured that her father had either been absent from the home when she was a child or else was very much a controller. I assumed that he was good at withholding affection from his daughter. How right I was! Her dad was one of those who never showed any affection or displayed any emotion because that wasn't the way men are supposed to act.

Lucy had an older brother and an older sister. Her older sister was little Miss Perfect who did almost everything right, while her brother was a top-notch athlete who had also been the president of his senior class in high school.

Lucy decided early in life that there was no way for her to be the best, so she might as well be the worst. She had found her niche by being truant from school, giving people a bad time, and basically giving her parents' strict moral values a good, strong kick in the teeth. She had a flippant attitude that said, "I'll never be serious about anything." It wasn't that she didn't care, but just that she didn't think anybody else would be interested in what she thought.

If they knew the things that were on her mind, they might make fun of her, and that was a risk that wasn't worth the trouble, so she hid behind a rough exterior that said, "I don't give a flip about anything."

During one of our sessions I told Lucy that she purposefully selected men who were no good for her, who would mistreat her and behave in an unloving manner toward her.

She was skeptical. "Why would anyone marry someone they knew would mistreat them?" I answered that many people would do just that because they were following the dictates of a lifestyle that says, "I'm not worth anything," and "I deserve to be abused," and "Nobody could possibly care about what *I* think!"

Through her lifestyle analysis, Lucy learned that one of the driving forces in her life was to get a man's attention, since she didn't have the attention of her father. It didn't make any difference if the attention she got from men was negative or positive, just as long as it was attention. It will not be an easy task to get Lucy to change her behavior or her perceptions of herself, but we are working on it.

I am confident that she is going to make it. She is going to begin to treat herself as a positive, loving person. She is going to learn that she has worthwhile things to say and important opinions to express. She won't have to continue to hide behind the mask that says, "I don't care about anything. Not even myself."

## No Success

The fourth reason why couples don't communicate is that they have never had any success at it. The husband has tried to tell his wife how he felt about something, but couldn't find the words to explain it in a way that she could understand. The wife wanted to tell her husband something that was of great importance to her, but right in the middle of it he started snoring like a buffalo with sinus problems. And so they both gave up and decided not to try again.

There are a number of reasons why husbands and wives have trouble communicating with each other, and one of the primary ones is that men and women tend to take different approaches to communication.

It is generally true that men take the approach of the journalist when it comes to communicating, whereas a woman is likely to be a storyteller. Now before you get upset with me and think that I'm saying women are liars, let me tell you that that isn't the implication of the term *storyteller*—not at all.

But before I get to that, let me explain what I mean by saying that men communicate like journalists. Every beginning newswriter knows that the most important elements of a story should be contained in the first paragraph, or the lead. These important elements are who, what, when, where, why, and sometimes how.

That's generally how a man likes to communicate, and it's the way he wants other people, including his wife, to communicate with him.

Now, the wife as a storyteller. A storyteller doesn't give away the climax of the story in the first paragraph. She wants to build suspense, to tell you how everything fell into place, and lead you gradually to the big conclusion.

The man may come home at the end of the day and say, "Johnson's department store burned to the ground this afternoon."

The woman may come home at the end of the day and tell you the same thing, but she'll start off by saying, "As I was leaving the office today, I thought I smelled smoke in the air. And then, sure enough—a couple of fire trucks went flying past, headed in the direction of Oak Street . . ."

Now remember that I'm not saying that all men communicate like journalists or that all women are storytellers, but there is a general tendency for the sexes to be divided along these lines. Do you think I'm wrong? Then why is it the wife who tends to "correct" her husband's version of things by reminding him of elements he's "forgotten"? (Elements that, more than likely, he left out on purpose to make his story more concise, which is another journalistic trait.) Now I am not saying that one approach to communication is correct and the other is wrong, but that

121

men and women need to understand these differences in communication styles.

The wife may feel shortchanged because her husband isn't giving her all the interesting details she craves. The husband may be impatient and say something unkind such as, "Will you *please* get to the point?"

But love overlooks the fact that your mate is not communicating something in the way you would choose to. And it is patient and gentle and encourages the other person to express himself in a way that is most comfortable to him.

Communication really is a complex entity. Many people have never had the opportunity to communicate with anyone in a deep and meaningful way. It's a sad commentary on the relationships we have with our mates, relatives, children, and friends. We spend too much time on frilly, surface communication, which adds no depth to any relationship.

There are basically two reasons why we have no success at good communication: (1) We don't listen, and (2) we don't perceive what is being said.

Listening is at least a third of the communication process, the other two-thirds being the sharing of self and the understanding that follows the listening. When your mate is talking to you and you are thinking about what you are going to say in response, then you are not listening. You are not really communicating because you're too busy formulating your own thoughts. This is especially true in arguments, where neither combatant is really listening to the points the other person is making. If there was more in the way of listening, there would be less in the way of disagreements.

What this bantering of words back and forth is doing is creating a competitive situation where somebody has to win and somebody has to lose. And it might even happen that nobody wins and *everybody* loses.

Always remember that a marriage is not a competition, and anything that tends to push it in that direction destroys the formula that says that "One Plus One Equals One."

## Five Levels of Communication

In one of the best books I've ever read about communication, *Why Am I Afraid to Tell You Who I Am?*, John Powell talks about the five levels of communication, which I want to discuss briefly.[3]

*The fifth level—cliché conversation.* The following little catch phrases are examples of this level of conversation: "Say, you're looking good." "You been keeping busy?" "How's the family?" There are many others, but I'm sure you get the idea. Just for the fun of it, here's something interesting you can try. The next time someone acknowledges you with a "Hi, how are you?" make a quick U-turn, walk up alongside him, and begin to tell him how you *really* are. The other person may turn different shades of the rainbow and may avoid you for the next few years, but at least you will have taken a step in the direction of genuine communication.

*The fourth level—reporting facts about others.* Ah! This is easy! These are words and conversations that are designed to keep us aloof and removed from people. We talk about others but avoid getting ourselves involved in the conversation in any personal way. It's easy and fun to talk about others. But then, of course, this can degenerate into gossip, and gossip is never good for anybody.

*The third level—ideas and judgments.* Here we begin to approach an area of real communication. At this level we are beginning to share our ideas, thoughts, and opinions. We still tend to be somewhat apprehensive and guarded, and if we meet with disapproval we may modify our opinions so that they are more to the other person's liking. At this level we are still most anxious to avoid conflict and criticism.

*The second level—feelings and emotions.* As husband and wife we begin to share the feelings that are underneath the ideas and opinions expressed. And far too many couples get to this level only rarely. For example, think of the husband who gets up and leaves the dinner table every night and never says anything to his wife about the meal or his appreciation for her efforts in fixing it. He has many opportunities to express his appreciation to his wife, but he lets them pass him by. He could say, simply, "Honey, that was a terrific dinner. You're a good cook, and I appreciate you," and it would make a world of difference to her. (But then, if he said something like that, he'd probably have to run and fetch the smelling salts.) There is a scene in *Fiddler on the Roof,* in which Tevye wants his wife, Golde, to tell him that she loves him. To his question of "Do you love me?" all she can reply is with a list of all the things she's done for him during their years of marriage. She's mended his clothes, she's cooked his meals, she's done this and that.

But still he persists, "Do you love me?"

You see, actions are not enough. Ever. Those innermost feelings of love and appreciation need to be given voice. I'm always hearing about how important it is for a woman to hear her man tell her how much he loves her, and that is very true. But don't think that the man doesn't need to hear his woman verbalize her feelings of love and appreciation for him, because he does.

On the other side of the ledger, it's also important to verbalize our frustration and anger—not in a bitter, condemning way, but in a way that doesn't block the lines of communication. Picture this situation: The wife is angry over something the husband has done, but he honestly hasn't a clue as to what it might have been.

"What's wrong?" he says.

"Nothing," comes the reply.

"I know something's wrong. Did I do something?"

"No . . . everything's fine." Although she says it in such a way that lets him know everything is most definitely *not* fine.

This kind of thing goes on all the time on the part of both husbands and wives, and it is very damaging to the marital relationship.

How much better it would be for that wife to say, "I am hurt because you walked in the door and spent ten minutes on the floor playing with the dog and didn't even acknowledge me," or to let her husband know whatever else is on her mind.

It is not easy to share all of our deepest emotions with another person—even if that person is someone we love enough to pledge our lives to. But little by little, step by step, we all need to move in the direction of:

*The first level—complete emotional and personal truthfulness* in communication. For us to survive in marriage this is a must. We have to develop an openness and honesty within our relationship that says, "I can tell you how I really feel without your judging that feeling." This level of communication is very difficult because of the possibility of being rejected.

For example, if the wife who thought her husband paid more attention to the dog than to her knew he would explode in anger if she told him how she felt, no wonder she wouldn't share her feelings with him. We all must strive to create an atmosphere in which an open and honest exchange is always encouraged and welcomed. But at the same time, remember that when your feelings have been hurt, you can express this in a nonaccusing manner. Chances are good that the person who hurt your feelings had no intention of doing so. And even if he did, it's always best to give the other person the benefit of the doubt.

Sometimes we hear things that weren't really said. We tend to filter the other person's conversation through our own biases, and it is wise not to try to read between the lines.

Honest does not mean rude. Nor does it mean blunt, or tactless, or an attitude of "I'm going to tell you something for your own good." Being honest does not mean that you have to "let it all hang out." Don't think that I'm advising you to go out and say, "You know, I've decided that I'm going to be totally honest with regard to my feelings, and I've got to tell you, I feel that you've got the most humongous nose I've ever seen."

There are some "feelings" that don't need to be expressed, ever, and you know what I'm talking about.

Now I know that communication is a difficult concept for us to master. Most of us stay at a superficial level. And yet, if I don't make an attempt to deal with the important things in life and in marriage on a strong, intimate communicative basis, then my mate is not going to enter into a risklike situation and share herself openly with me. We will never become one.

Right alongside this problem of communication lies another—the inability to express our emotions in an acceptable, satisfying way. That's next up for discussion.

## Action, Not Words

One way you can start to increase communication in your marriage is to do the following exercise. Find a time when you can simply sit back and listen to your mate. Don't interrupt and don't think about what you are going to say. Just simply listen. Then communicate verbally and nonverbally that you really understand what your mate is trying to say. Reinforce that you are interested and that you care enough to listen in depth.

Another exercise I frequently give to couples who come for marital help is to have them sit facing each other and then discuss a subject I give them. One person begins to tell the other person how he or she really feels about the matter, and the other person is not free to interrupt. Then, when the first person has finished talking, the other person has the task of capsulizing what has just been said. The first speaker either affirms, denies, or modifies what he or she meant and what the other person heard. Then the roles are reversed. A little bit of practice in this type of communication will soon make you aware of how you may misconstrue things that your mate is trying to say, or how your mate may be misinterpreting your comments. This is an excellent way to improve speaking and listening skills.

# 6

## Nothing More Than Feelings

In this chapter, I want you to learn five things about feelings:

1. Your feelings aren't right or wrong.
2. You have a right to express them.
3. You don't always have to act on them.
4. You should never ask your mate, "Why do you feel that way?" (Because that places the emphasis on the cause and not the feeling.)
5. Feelings draw you closer to your mate, but judgments push you apart.

Let me say that all of us have feelings. Sometimes we get those feelings trampled on. Sometimes we trample on the feelings of others. Most of us have learned not to share our feelings, and probably all of us can recall experiences where we did reveal them and somebody was there to pounce on us for doing so.

When we start out in life, we're painfully honest about the way we feel—too honest in many instances.

For example, I remember the time when my own son, Kevin, was two years old and we had a couple over for dinner. Just as we were beginning to enjoy the meal, Kevy turned to his mother and asked, "Mommy, what's her name?"

Sande turned adoringly toward our son and answered, "That's Mrs. McVay."

"Oh," he said. "I hate her."

Apparently that was a new word he had learned that day. At any rate, he was certainly free with *his* feelings. I'm not advocating that any of us should be that open with what's in our hearts, but most of us have gone much too far in the other direction. We can't tell anyone how we feel without checking first to see in which direction the wind is blowing.

I've even talked to married couples who have let this unwillingness to express feelings invade their bedrooms. They're snuggling into bed at night, and he's kind of interested, and so's she, but neither one of them is quite sure how the other one feels.

He reaches over and gives her a love pat.

"Well . . . uh . . . good night," he says. "Love you."

"Love you too, honey."

They lie there for a moment and then she reaches over and pats him.

"You feeling okay?" she asks.

"Oh, yeah . . . sure. You?"

"Fine."

Another couple of moments of silence, and then he asks, "Are you, ah . . . you know . . . uh . . . interested . . . ?"

"Well . . . yeah, sure . . . I guess. . . ."

"Unless you're too tired . . ."

"Oh, I'm not *that* tired. But if *you* are, it's okay, because I'm *kind* of tired. . . ."

And they go on like that for a while until they fall asleep, exhausted from all the dancing around the subject.

Am I exaggerating? Maybe a little. But from what I've heard over the years from my clients, not very much.

In this instance, the husband can't bring himself to express his feelings to his wife, to say, "I love you, and I want to make love to you." And the wife won't tell her husband that the thing she wants right now, more than anything else, is for him to hold her in his arms. And so they go without what they really want.

We simply must learn to communicate with each other, to share our feelings in all areas of life.

Now, let's take an up-close look at those five things I told you that I want you to learn in this chapter.

## Your Feelings Aren't Right or Wrong

A feeling isn't something that stems from the intellect. You don't say, "This person has said something bad about me so I think I'm going to feel hurt for a while." If somebody has said something bad about you, you're automatically going to be hurt. That's just the way it is. A feeling is an emotional reaction that exists within you, whether you want it to exist or not, whether you like the feeling or not. Having negative feelings does not make you a bad person, nor does having positive feelings make you a good person.

As I mentioned earlier, sometimes the natural inclination to show our feelings is beaten out of us early in life. We are taught not to be rude, not to hurt people, not to get too excited, not to express too much affection, not to grieve, not to cry. As we grow more "mature" we may choose to intellectualize and rationalize why we can't or don't share our feelings. It's easier, we discover, to be a plastic person than a real one. Since we are not used to sharing our emotions, or seeing other people share theirs, there is a distinct danger that we might be misunderstood.

For example, if I make this statement, "I think you are very beautiful," you might react with one of these thoughts: "I feel inferior to you"; "I feel ugly"; "This fellow is trying to manipulate me because he wants something from me"; or "I wonder what he's up to"; or any of several other reactions. Perhaps my words were intended as an honest compliment, but that's only one of many possible ways you could perceive them.

If I am afraid that my comment will trigger any of these negative reactions within you, I might rationalize, "I'd better not express how I feel about her or else I might cause some problems to come between us." When the person you are interacting with in that way is your wife or your husband, then you are leaving your marriage wide open to destruction.

What happens when we repress our feelings? In one way or another, we pay for it. Many of the people I see in my private practice suffer from things such as gastro-intestinal disorders, headaches, backaches, back spasms, muscle spasms . . . and all sorts of other problems, because they have chosen to repress their feelings. These repressed emotions have then begun to express themselves physiologically.

Remember that you cannot help how you feel, and you have no reason to apologize for your feelings. If I have negative feelings toward you and I act them out in a hostile and harmful way, then I have to be held accountable for my actions. But there is nothing wrong with the feelings in and of themselves.

## You Have a Right to Express Your Feelings

Since your emotions are neither right nor wrong, you have a right to express them. But what happens when you want to sit down and share and you meet the great wall of resistance?

I think of Betty Jane, twenty-four, who had tried on numerous occasions to express her feelings of neglect, worry, frustration, fear, and anger about her nonrelationship with her husband. Every time she began to express her feelings, he would tromp right over them and tell her in no uncertain terms to "get off my case."

Finally, at my urging, Betty Jane wrote her husband a personal love letter and sent it to his place of business. He wouldn't listen to her when she tried to approach him on a verbal basis but my hope, and hers, was that he would at least pay attention to her written words.

The letter worked. He read it. He seemed to understand, and it began the process of enabling this young couple to communicate with each other.

If you can't express yourself verbally, or if your mate or other loved one won't listen to you, then I heartily recommend that you take the time to sit down and write a letter.

One word of caution, though. If you start it off with "Dear Banana-Nose," you stand the risk of not being heard. I am jesting here, of course, but my point is that the letter needs to say what you want to say in as gentle and palatable a way as possible. What you want to do here is open the door to the possibility of better communication, not slam it shut.

And if your mate is opening up his innermost feelings to you, try your hardest to be sensitive. Some people can't handle the discomfort they feel when they are forced to deal with true human emotion. I know people who cannot handle others sharing their grief, for instance. If a friend has lost a loved one, for example, it is totally wrong to brush him off with some statement such as, "It's time to get on with your life," or "God always knows best."

How much better it is to put your arm around the grieving person and cry with him—or just tell him that you care. It's a sad commentary on our society when we're afraid to reach out and touch people. It's pathetic when someone reaches out to us and we respond with a denial of feelings, both theirs and our own.

How do you begin to share your own feelings so you can understand the feelings of those around you? One way is to be willing to take the time to sit and talk with each other. We cannot read each other's minds, though we often insist we can. There are times when you have to tell, and there are times when you have to ask. Begin today to share your feelings, and be especially sensitive to and encourage your children's and your mate's expressions of honest emotions.

## YOU DON'T ALWAYS HAVE TO ACT ON YOUR FEELINGS

Although we have the capacity to experience a full range of feelings, it is important to realize that we can choose not to act on them. This would be a terrible world if we all went around acting out our feelings. In psychological terms we refer to the libidinous forces that are running around inside of us as the "id." The id is the portion of the personality that drives us to act on impulse.

Just imagine what would happen if we all acted on impulse!

Some guy cuts in front of you in traffic? No problem. Just pull out a gun and blow him away. (And you may remember how frequently that was happening on the freeways of Los Angeles a few years ago.) Your neighbor's dog has left a present on your lawn—again? No problem here either. Just dump your cat's litter box all over his front porch. Laurel and Hardy once starred in a film called *Tit for Tat,* in which one small act of violence led to another, and that to another, and so on, in an escalating spiral, until an entire house was completely demolished. If we all acted impulsively on our feelings, our entire society would collapse just as that house did.

Many years ago, I knew a young man who was so fiercely competitive on the baseball field that he threw temper tantrums. As a man in his early twenties he was ejected from many ball games for throwing his bat, kicking the dirt, stomping his feet, and cussing out umpires. He was overdriven with the desire to be terribly competitive. He felt he *had* to win. He allowed his feelings to get the best of him. Not only did they surface, but they dominated him during the entire ball game. It got to the point where his teammates tiptoed around him and did their best to avoid him altogether.

During the 1991 major league season, Cincinnati Reds pitcher Rob Dibble, who was widely regarded as one of the best pitchers in the business, announced that he would seek counseling to help him keep his feelings under control. This was after, among several other incidents, he threw a ball into the stands in anger, hitting and injuring a spectator, and then hit a base runner in the back of the legs with a thrown ball. He said the base runner incident was a case where the ball "got away from him," but those who knew him seriously doubted that version of things.

He had a chance to be one of the all-time greats of major league baseball, but it never happened because he couldn't keep his emotions under control.

Acting out feelings in this fashion is often a controlling type of behavior. It's usually true that when we let our feelings rise to the top in this way, we're doing it for a purpose. We often get our own way through being powerful, explosive, or—going in the other direction—by choosing to withdraw, being sheepish or moody. An example of the "quiet-type" controller is the "depressed" wife who complains all the time about not getting enough attention. What she is really doing is exercising a neurotic type of attention-getting. This is her way of keeping her mate's toe right there on that line.

I've talked to people who admitted that they had acted unwisely, but who would then defend themselves by saying, "That's just the way I am and there's not much I can do about it." Wrong. That person is saying, "I refuse to change. I'm not even going to try." And that's unfortunate.

You may feel angry and as though you want to punch someone in the nose, and it's okay to feel that way, but it's also important to find a way to express those feelings in an acceptable manner.

Now suppose that in a restaurant a waitress is extremely rude to you. You may feel put out about it, and you may consider reporting your anger to the waitress or to the manager. One way to express the way you feel is simply not to leave a tip. But you're not handling the situation very well if you trip her the next time she passes by with a tray of food or dishes, or if you take a poke at her as you're on your way out of the restaurant.

Again, you need to find an acceptable and constructive way to express your feelings—especially within the framework of marriage, where it's important to express your feelings in as nonthreatening and loving a way as possible.

In the Bible, the Book of Ephesians has some solid advice when it urges its readers to "not let the sun go down while you are still angry" (Eph. 4:26). In other words, don't go to bed with unexpressed feelings toward your mate.

Let him know how you feel and don't leave unresolved problems hanging in the air. Deal with the problem now, and you'll be much better off tomorrow.

One final thought: Although it's important to know how you feel, it's more important to realize that feelings change, therefore you can't run your life by your feelings! Suppose someone cuts you off in traffic. Getting in touch with your feelings might mean getting into an accident. It's better to rise above your feelings and do the right thing.

## A QUESTION YOU NEVER ASK

Why do I say you should never ask your mate, "Why do you feel that way?"

Primarily because this question provides the groundwork for immediate resistance and defensiveness. The word *why* can be a stopper that puts an immediate end to conversation. If you really want to know how your mate feels, you have to be willing to devote some time to honest dialogue. A "why" question is an intrusion into your mate's thoughts and feelings and can prohibit you from hearing feelings that are of a deeper origin.

Asking "why" takes you away from an accepting environment and puts you in a judgmental posture. In order to judge someone you have to be superior, and a marriage is a relationship of two equals.

For example, Marcy tried to listen with good humor and acceptance to the many wonderful things her husband had to say about his secretary, Bonnie. Finally, though, she just couldn't take it anymore and decided to tell him how she felt. John listened to about three sentences and then shook his head.

"Why do you feel that way?" he said.

Marcy ran from the room in tears; end of conversation but certainly not the end of the problem.

John's "why" question was saying, in essence, "Your reaction is totally uncalled for. It's completely incomprehensible to me."

Even if John had thought Marcy's jealousy was unfounded, he should have said something along the lines of, "Honey, I'm sorry you feel that way. I don't mean to hurt your feelings. Let's talk about it." His response shouldn't have been to become defensive and pooh-pooh his wife's feelings but rather to spend some time reinforcing the fact that his deepest love and respect were reserved for her and her alone, not for his secretary.

If you really know your mate as you should, you probably already know the answer to the "why" question. In Marcy's case it was because (a) her husband had too many good things to say about his secretary; (b) she loved him and was afraid that another woman might be coming between them; and (c) she needed reassurance that she had the top spot in her husband's life.

As for Marcy, she didn't stop to think, "I'm going to be jealous"; she just was. Remember what we said earlier, that feelings do not stem from the intellect but from the emotions.

You don't have to agree with everything your mate says. If you did, that would soon lead to a totally dull relationship. But, out of respect and love, you should listen to each other, value each other's opinions, and seek to work out a solution to any problems.

To sum it up, the reasons to refrain from asking "why" are:

1. It inhibits communication.
2. It implies the need to defend our feelings.
3. It inhibits acceptance.
4. It triggers defensiveness.

## FEELINGS DRAW YOU CLOSER, JUDGMENTS PUSH YOU APART

One of the reasons we have trouble understanding our own or our mate's feelings is that we layer those feelings with judgments, opinions, and values, or we blame someone else for giving us those feelings. As in: "She makes me so mad!" "That guy drives me crazy." Or even, "You made me love you."

Statements such as these are examples of how we project another person as the source of our own anger or other emotions. The fact is that your feelings are made, manufactured, and distributed by your own self. Anger, joy, happiness, fear—every emotion comes from within you.

The next time you have to wait in a long line, take a look around you and see how the other people in the line are reacting. Some will obviously be angry and even talking to those around them. "This is ridiculous! I can't believe we have to wait in this line. Who do they think they are?" All that sort of thing. And yet other folks will be calm, collected, even serene. It's an inconvenience, yes, but it's not the end of the world.

If you listen to what's being said, you're likely to find that the angry people are the ones who are blaming someone else for this problem: "They have no right to make us wait like this." "They should be better organized." "Who do they think they are?" And so on. Those who aren't angry aren't assessing blame. They're just thinking, "Well, these things happen sometimes, so I might as well make the best of the situation."

Am I saying that it's wrong to get angry? No, we all get angry at times, and our anger may be justified. All I'm saying is that you need to understand where your emotions come from and quit assessing blame for them.

Try to begin expressing yourself with "I" statements rather than "you" or "they" statements. The idea is to say,

"I feel very angry when you say things like that." In this way, you are focusing first on your response rather than upon the other person's actions.

H. Norman Wright, in his book *The Pillars of Marriage,* says that "there are four main ways to describe feelings verbally: 1) Identify or name the feeling. 'I feel angry'; 'I feel sad'; 'I feel good about you.' 2) Use similes and metaphors. . . . 'I feel squelched'; 'I felt like a cool breeze going through the air.' 3) Report the type of action your feelings urge you to do. 'I feel like hugging you'; 'I wish I could hit you.' 4) Use figures of speech, such as, 'The sun is smiling on me today'; 'I feel like a dark cloud is following me around today.'"[4]

Learning to express your feelings and recognizing that nobody but you is responsible for them will help you to stop being judgmental. And a marriage is in big trouble if both partners are blaming each other for the way they feel. Think how fulfilling it would be if you could tell your mate your frustrations, concerns, and fears, and know that he wouldn't judge or condemn you. You might even soften the sharing of your feelings by saying, "I'm not sure why I feel this way . . . but right now I'm feeling hurt . . ." or angry . . . or left out . . . or whatever way you might be feeling.

Unfortunately too many of us are what I call "bone-diggers." What I mean by this is that long after the specific event is over and after all the dust has settled, if true emotions and feelings have never been expressed, the "bone-digger" may dig up those bones of long-gone emotions. Such an exercise is rarely productive. If you are the person who is always bringing up the misdeeds of the past, that may soon be where your marriage lies—in the past.

If your marital relationship is not based upon openness and honesty, then chances are good that your relationship will be adolescent-like, where all the manifestations of adolescence—jealousy, accusations, bantering back and forth, pouting, getting mad, leaving in a huff, etc.—are evident. Those kinds of behaviors will be found in relationships that are stagnant and going nowhere—and not in a thriving marriage.

## THE IMPORTANCE OF TRUST

As a psychologist, I always take the time to tell my clients about myself. I tell them that I am married, that I have a lovely wife and five children, that I enjoy family therapy and private practice, that I'm action-oriented, and that my true mission in life is to "get rid of my clients." I see that getting rid of them is an encouraging process that says they don't have to be dependent on me to make progress.

I begin to share with them my unique self. I usually mention that I graduated near the bottom of my high school class and couldn't get admitted to college—I applied to over one hundred of them unsuccessfully. (I eventually got into one; sorry, I can't give you the name—we have a working agreement. . . .) I share some of the inadequacies I feel as a person, some of the fears I have, some of my priorities in life. And I begin to share with them real experiences that I think might be helpful for them to hear.

I don't share my deepest feelings during our first meeting, but I try to plant the seed that it's okay for us to talk about anything, and that I'm going to be involved in our discussions. I am not going to be some far-off object who, every five minutes, is going to make a "significant" contribution by nodding my head and saying, "Uh-huh. Uh-huh." I tell my clients that I expect to be honest with them, and I want them to be honest with me. And if we are going to take the time and trouble to be honest with each other, to share our thoughts and feelings, our hidden frustrations, hurts, and angers, then I have to be brave enough to accept their feelings and lay the groundwork for constructive, helpful advice.

This kind of a relationship is necessary before a psychologist and his client can begin to work on the problem. And if this sort of relationship is important to the psychologist-client relationship, just think how important it must be to a relationship as significant as that found within a marriage. It is vitally important that we open up and show our true selves to our spouses and that we accept our spouse's emotions without feeling threatened or being judgmental.

For us to be successful in therapy, in life, or in marriage, we really must learn to trust each other. Trust is telling the other person who you really are and being willing to share your most intimate thoughts and feelings. It's like handing your mate a jewelry box full of precious stones and saying, "Here are my feelings. I'm going to share them with you because I know you'll take care of them. You won't dump them in the dirt, or step on them, or throw them in the trash."

Remember too, that sharing your feelings with your mate is not a one-shot deal. It's a continual process of unraveling the mystery of each individual. Every day we are changing, perceiving different things, and developing different attitudes and feelings about life, and every day we must be willing to discuss these changes with our mates.

Begin today to share your feelings. And as you do, listen for words that might indicate you are blaming someone else for your feelings. If and when that happens, apologize for it, retreat, gather up your thoughts and feelings again, and then go forward. It's not always going to be a rose garden, but if you begin to honestly share your feelings with your mate and to be supportive and understanding of his feelings, you'll soon find that your relationship has hit a new high. You'll have a higher awareness of your love for each other and you'll be moving closer to the ideal in marriage. *Acceptance* is what happens after you have shared your feelings.

# 7

## Women Are from Pluto and Men Are a Bit Goofy Too

Thirty years ago we put a man on the moon. We've made great technological advances in the last generation. Soon we'll all have telephones on our *watches,* for goodness' sake. And yet in this day of enlightenment, in this time of scientific genius, in this era of general brilliance, men still don't understand women and women still don't understand men.

All right, we're getting better. Men seem to be trying harder these days. A decade ago, only about 10 percent of the audience at my marriage seminars was male. Now it's about half. Women have traditionally been better at understanding the opposite sex, but now many are realizing they don't know as much about men as they think they do. In spite of our best efforts, the two genders still seem pretty mysterious to each other.

So here's a news flash for you: MEN AND WOMEN ARE DIFFERENT!

Duh. I know that's been obvious to you since your preschool days, but this simple truth is far more profound than it sounds. God made us different! I think it shows God's sense of humor. He could have made us entirely alike. Life would be simpler that way . . . and probably much more boring. Instead, he gave us different bodies with different chemistries, different minds with different personalities, different characteristics and different needs.

Our society has spent a couple of decades pretending this isn't true. It was feared that if you start saying men are like *this* and women are like *that,* then men will assume they're better than women, or vice versa. So we weren't allowed to say anything about the differences, but still we all knew they were there. Whenever women traipsed off to the ladies' room *together,* like a covey of quail, even asking *others* to go *with* them, men realized that they were dealing with a completely different species. Whenever a man drove through three counties, completely lost but *not* asking for directions, his wife had to wonder what planet he came from.

Not long ago I had to take our six-year-old, Lauren, to the dentist, but I had never been there before. I asked Sande for directions and this is exactly what she told me: "You can't miss it. Right in the front of the office are some beautiful flower beds, but don't go in the front door. That looks like his office but it's not. Go in the side entrance."

That was it. The street name, the address, how to get there—none of that was important. I could go driving all day looking for "beautiful flower beds" right in front of a front door that's not the entrance! But that illustrates a difference in the way Sande and I think, and the same is true for many husbands and wives. Sande had a lovely memory of the front of the dentist's office, and she was concerned that I go in the right doorway. That's all very nice, but I'm a guy! I need coordinates! Give me an address and I'll hunt that puppy down, I'll bag it, I'll put a bow around it—but tell me *where!*

Even when we weren't supposed to admit the differences between the sexes, whenever anyone asked directions, we *knew.* We knew.

The popular book *Men Are from Mars, Women Are from Venus* by John Gray, along with myriad sequels and seminars, has helped to bring our culture back to its senses. But numerous marriage books (including my own) have been saying the same thing all along: MEN AND WOMEN ARE DIFFERENT! NOT BETTER, NOT WORSE. JUST DIFFERENT! GET OVER IT!

The challenge in every marriage is to recognize these differences, to understand them, and to fit them together so the couple can function as a team. That's what God had in mind all along. Not a "battle of the sexes" that one or the other would "win," but a relationship where both would express their love fully and grow together in their commitment to one another.

Imagine listening to a barbershop quartet and later paying this compliment to the baritone: "Congratulations! I think you won. Your voice was much better than the other three singers. It stood out strongly and made it clear that you're the best musician." Though you're intending to encourage him, the singer does not look happy. His voice wasn't supposed to stand out. It wasn't a competition. They were creating harmony, different notes combining in beautiful chords.

It's the same thing with marriage. Maybe, just maybe, God the creator had this great idea—that masculine and feminine could combine in this unique relationship and make sweet music together.

## DRIVING US TO OUR NEEDS

Marriage revolves around a simple little word called *needs*. As a marriage counselor and psychologist, I'm often asked the secret of a successful marriage. In a world torn apart by divorce, people want to know how to make their marriages work. Well, here's the answer: Become an expert in meeting your spouse's needs. In successful marriages, each partner works to meet the other's needs.

Now you should know in advance that you're not going to meet *all* the needs of your mate, no matter what the popular books tell you. You're going to fail at meeting some of those needs. A good spouse doesn't expect the other to bat 1,000. But you need to get the bat off your shoulder, at least. You need to work at meeting a good number of your spouse's needs as best you can.

In order to meet them, you need to know what they are. And that's where most couples get into trouble. When they say their vows, they fully intend "to have and to hold" and all the rest, but somewhere down deep they assume that their spouse's needs will be pretty much like their own. He assumes that she needs a roof over her head, maybe a really nice roof, with matching furniture, grocery money, an occasional vacation, and a wide-screen TV—and so he'll do his part to provide those things. She assumes that he needs long moonlit walks, fireside chats, hugs, and kids. After all, he seemed to love all that stuff when they were dating.

But now he's sprawled out on the couch watching the Green Bay Packers on his big-screen TV, and she's perched on the matching chair wanting to talk about their relationship. What's her problem? What's his problem? What's wrong with this picture?

Her needs and his needs are very different. A marriage won't thrive until both partners realize that.

## HIS NEEDS

What's the #1 need for a man in a marriage?
Affirmation? It's important, but not the top need.
Communication? Get real!
Sex? Now you're talking . . . but this isn't exactly right either. Most women think that most men are "after only one thing," but that's far too simplistic. The #1 need is not sex, but *sexual fulfillment*. There's a heck of a difference.

A man's sexual need is far more than just physical. It's also mental and, believe it or not, emotional. A lot of wives don't realize this about their husbands. (Frankly, a lot of husbands don't realize this about themselves.) Couples develop sexual problems when they both view sex as merely a physical thing. Both of them need to use their creativity to make it a more fulfilling experience.

To meet this need, both partners need to pay a lot of attention to each other. You have very different bodies, with different rhythms, different ways of receiving sexual pleasure, and different things that excite you. To achieve sexual fulfillment, ideally both partners should be satisfied.

But let me go off on a tangent here. I've heard too many women complain, "My husband doesn't believe in showering or washing his hands or brushing his teeth. How am I supposed to enjoy sex with a man like that?" Good question. Guys, you have to pay attention to basic hygiene. As you come to bed with your wife, think of it as a date with her and fix yourself up as you used to when you were dating her. If this has been a problem for you, a few simple measures will go a long way to improving your sexual relationship.

There are two other major men's needs I want to discuss. One is *respect*. Maybe there's an ego gene carried on the Y chromosome, I don't know—but men need to know they're important. I'm not condoning all the rude and violent things some men do to salvage their pride, but men do feel a need for respect more than women do. In fact, many of men's most oafish displays of pride occur because they feel they're not getting enough respect.

So, wives, do not badmouth your husband in front of the kids. And do not share your marital frustrations over a café latte with the neighborhood gossip. If you truly want to succeed in your marriage, show some respect. Affirm your husband whenever possible. Let him know you think he's the greatest thing since microwave popcorn.

A third basic need of men is *the need to be needed.* As you can see, these three all fit together. A man feels important when he's needed, and there's a sexual satisfaction that comes from knowing you're pleasing your wife. As a man who's been married thirty-two years, I get much more pleasure out of watching my wife enjoy me than I do getting my own physical satisfaction. It's great to know that she needs me, and that I'm meeting those needs. I feel that I'm fulfilling my purpose in life.

The modern feminist movement had a saying: "A woman needs a man like a fish needs a bicycle." It's funny, and it properly strikes out at anyone who would say women are inferior to men—but it's wrong. Let me rephrase it this way: Wives need husbands like fish need water, and husbands need wives the same way.

I'm not saying that a wife has to act like a helpless waif every time she needs to open a jar. But wives should let their husbands know what they need and praise them to high heaven when they meet those needs.

## HER NEEDS

Now can you guess the #1 need of women?

"Visa," said one man when I asked that question at a recent marriage seminar. I think I saw his wife elbow him.

More than anything, women need *affection*. Hugs, kisses, handholding, backrubs. But *not* sex. They need affection *as* affection, not just foreplay. They don't need to be grabbed. Yes, I know many men who are world-class grabbers, but I've yet to meet a woman who says, "I just love it when my husband grabs me." Women need to be petted, caressed, embraced.

You see, guys, there's one question that your wife needs to have answered every day: *Do you really love me?* You can answer that question in many ways, with words as well as hugs, caresses, and so on. But these physical actions only seem like love *if they have nothing to do with sex*. If your wife thinks you're only kissing her to get her into bed, she won't feel truly loved. And if a husband seems to be interested only in sex, any wife is going to feel used.

Of course, this need for affection doesn't always fit well with the #1 need of men—sexual fulfillment. But sometimes it does, and if a couple can find a way to merge these two needs, they've got a great thing going.

Don't forget, though, that affection can be shown in a million ways. For instance, taking out the garbage without being asked can be foreplay. Think about it. And if, as my colleague and friend Gary Smalley says, men are microwaves and women are crockpots, the crockpots will get colder and colder if men do not practice courtesy and hygiene, and if they engage in verbal abuse, condescending attitudes, and angry outbursts.

In a way, that's the theme of this whole book. If you practice a lifestyle of affection, that should create sexual fulfillment as well. Sex does begin in the kitchen.

There's a second set of needs for women that many men find difficult to fulfill. *Honesty. Openness. Communication.*

Recent scientific studies have shown that women tend to have more connecting fibers than men have between the verbal side of their brains and the emotional side. That's why they're so good at expressing their feelings and . . . well, that's why men grunt a lot.

"How was your day at work, dear?"

"Gffnnnrr."

"What does that mean?"

It means he's not ready to talk about his day at work. Those feelings haven't yet traveled over to his speech center. Remember: *Her* feelings are zipping along an eight-lane superhighway while his are poking along a little dirt road. They'll get there, eventually. In the meantime, he can only focus on basic human needs.

"What's for dinner? Did you put carrots in the pot roast?"

Wives need to understand their husbands' lack of communication, but they don't have to settle for it. Communication is the lifeblood of any relationship, and husbands need to step up to this challenge. Still, wives may need to wait for the right time, as their husbands' feelings finally chug into the conversational zone.

I find that many men have no trouble talking about Mark McGwire's batting average or the size of the trout they caught last summer. They'll discuss in detail the capabilities of their car engine or the best way to put up drywall. They'll quote you stock prices or interest rates. But how do they *feel* about their jobs, their future, their families? The emotional stuff is tough.

Unfortunately, their wives don't know McGwire from McMuffins, and stock prices put them to sleep. Emotions are what they care about. That's their turf.

So husbands need to take a chance, stepping out into unfamiliar territory. If you're really committed to meeting your wife's needs, you have to reach down for your feelings and put them out there on the table. That's what she needs.

It may not be pretty, but that's okay. You may wind up saying something like, "I'm not sure how I feel about that.

152

I think I feel that maybe I'm kind of excited about my job promotion, but I'm kind of scared too, in a way, and I don't want to get my hopes up. You know what I mean?"

Granted, that doesn't sound like John Updike's prose (well, actually it *does* sound like Updike prose), but it does the job. And the great thing is that she *does* know what you mean. Or if she doesn't, she'll ask. And, hey, you're communicating. She feels that you love her enough to share your soul with her. Don't you want to do that?

A third thing many wives need from their husbands is *commitment to the family.* It's true that sometimes children can get in the way of marital intimacy, but generally a woman feels comforted and loved when her husband spends meaningful time with the kids.

Unfortunately, many men still pursue the role of the uninvolved breadwinner. They work eighty hours a week to make good money so they can buy a spiffy house in an upscale neighborhood—but they never see the family that lives there! They may crash in front of the TV late at night or crawl into bed next to their wives, but they're not really part of the family life. That's not their job, as they see it.

As a result, these men are strangers to their families. The moms do the child-rearing (even though they're often working full-time too). Maybe the dads make occasional guest appearances to mete out discipline, hand out allowances, or to assist in major family decisions, but they're not part of the day-to-day workings of the home.

Granted, it's tough to be a dad. Most women seem to have a natural connection with children, while men have to work extra hard to understand their children's needs. But child-rearing is a skill that has to be learned, like anything else. Fathers need to make a commitment to study this subject, to ride the learning curve, and most of all to take the time necessary to become the world's experts on their own children's development. If they're there for the launching, they need to be there for the landing.

Fortunately, dads these days are getting much, much better. And mothers breathe easier knowing that fathers care about the kids.

## Talk about It

Always be careful when a book tells you what your marriage needs. Including this one. I've given you generalities. Chances are, you and your spouse have most of the six needs I mentioned, but you may be an exception, or the needs may be in a different order.

My point is that you need to talk about your own needs. Discuss the needs I've mentioned. What would give him more sexual fulfillment? What expressions of affection does she like the most? But then look at the other side too. How could she find more sexual fulfillment? What kinds of hugs and caresses does he like?

How can she show him more respect? How can he feel that he's needed? How and when can the couple communicate better? What can be done to create a safe environment for openness and honesty? How can he demonstrate his commitment to the family?

Consider other needs as well. In *His Needs, Her Needs,* Willard Harley mentions other marital needs such as recreational companionship, domestic support, financial support, and the need for an attractive spouse. How do these needs rate in your marriage? Are there other needs that are especially important to you?

As I've said, your success or failure in marriage depends on how good you are at knowing your spouse's needs and meeting them. So communicate your own needs and pay attention to your spouse's needs.

When counseling people with marital troubles, I occasionally hear them confessing that they're having extramarital affairs. You'd be amazed how often they say something like, "You won't believe this, Doctor, but it's not about sex." I do believe it, because I've heard it again and again. People find in an affair whatever's lacking in their marriage. If they're not feeling sexually fulfilled in marriage, yes, they'll seek sex elsewhere. But more often the unmet needs in marriage are things like conversation, respect, or emotional support, and those are the things that straying spouses often find in the company of other lovers.

I'm not excusing affairs, just explaining them. Affairs are about unmet needs. When you neglect your spouse's most important needs, you send him or her elsewhere for fulfillment.

What's the answer? Make sure your marriage is everything it can be. Satisfied partners don't wander. If you become the expert in meeting your spouse's most important needs, why would they look in any other direction?

## BEHIND HER EYES

Of course, sometimes you have to be a mind reader.

Our family took a weekend trip out to California to see the Arizona Wildcats play football. As we drove, Sande asked if I wanted to stop for a cup of coffee. I said no and drove on.

There was silence from the passenger side for two minutes. As we neared an exit, Sande screamed (lovingly, of course), "I WANT A CUP OF COFFEE AND I WANT IT NOW!"

What happened there? First of all, you have to understand my mindset. We're on the road, and that means my male computer has already determined the mileage, our average speed, a reasonable number of stops, and a projected time of arrival. I want to make good time.

Meanwhile, my wife has decided she wants to stop. She doesn't want to demand it; she wants to suggest it, and she does so by appealing to my needs. According to Sande's female logic, I should register the fact that she's asking, and I should ask *her* if *she* wants to stop, or I should just assume that she does. In other words, I should read her mind.

But my male logic doesn't make all those jumps. I'm a linear thinker. She asks me a direct question, and I give her a direct answer. What's the problem? Besides, I want to keep driving.

The problem is that I should know better. As a husband, I ought to be so tuned in to my wife's needs that I know when a simple question is a suggestion. I need to get "behind her eyes" to know what she's thinking.

I'm not the only one. A man came up to me the second day of a seminar and said, "You know, Dr. Leman, I really didn't want to come to this, but my wife dragged me here. It's pretty good, though."

Nice to get a compliment, especially from a man. "But I've got a question," he went on. "On the way home last night, my wife asked if I wanted to stop for ice cream, and I said no. By the time we got home, my wife was mad. Hopping mad. At me. I finally figured out she was mad because we didn't stop for ice cream. But I don't get it."

I smiled and said, "You failed last night's session. I give you a big F."

"What are you talking about?"

"Remember how we said that your wife wants you to read her mind? It's not just that she wanted ice cream. She wanted to know that you understood her! That's what made her mad. It's not Baskin-Robbins she wants, it's you."

Sometimes this is challenging. Women often demand that men understand things even Einstein couldn't decipher. It takes work to figure it out sometimes. Husbands often find it easier to play dumb (or to *be* dumb) rather than make the effort to understand. "If she really wants something," we think, "she'll come right out and say it." But the effort is the whole point. Are you willing to do the work required to understand your wife a level beyond words? That's what she wants.

Men can be hard to understand too. Even though our communication tends to be pretty direct, we often withhold information if we're not asked directly. Women need to get behind the eyes of their husbands too, if only to know what questions to ask.

Let's say Frank really wants to meet his wife's needs. He comes home Friday with a great idea. The kids get farmed out to various friends, relatives, or church activities, and he whispers to his wife those three little words she loves to hear . . . "out to dinner."

So they get in the car, and she's all excited. "Where are we going?" she asks.

He really hadn't thought this far ahead.

"Is it a surprise?" she asks again.

"Well, sort of," he says. It's a surprise to him that this matters so much. I mean, there are a zillion restaurants out there. Take your pick. "Where would you like to go?" he says gallantly.

"Oh, I don't care," she says. "Surprise me."

She may not even realize it, but she's testing him. Does he know her well enough to pick a place she'd like?

Frank, meanwhile, is thinking, "She said she doesn't care, so it's up to me." And he swings the car into Taco Bell. Hey, all the burritos you can eat for only . . .

And she thinks, "Oh, my! What a surprise!"

She may have said she doesn't care, but she does. What she meant was that she doesn't want to order him around. She wants him to choose a place he knows *she* would like. Not Taco Bell.

Frank scored points with his "out to dinner" plan. But Taco Bell cost him, big time. And it has nothing to do with the quality of the food or how much it cost. It just shows that he has no clue about *her.* He doesn't care enough to study her likes and dislikes. She wants him to understand her, and he doesn't.

If I'm going to be a good husband, I have to get behind my wife's eyes. If my main job on this earth is to help meet her needs, I have to know what those needs are. I have to learn how to think as she thinks, what kinds of things she'll like or dislike, what she really wants—even if she's not putting her desires into words.

When you were dating, you put a lot of work into pleasing the other person. You polished yourself up, presenting yourself as the most desirable person you could be. You probably went places with your date you wouldn't have gone yourself—but you wanted to share in the life of this exciting new person. You worked hard to get to know this person, learning what gifts, what words, what activities he or she preferred.

Well, you married that person, and you got to know your spouse even better in the first few years of marriage. But often your spouse becomes like a beautiful gold coin you find on the ground somewhere. It's beautiful! It's great! You love it! You brag about it to your friends! You treasure it! But eventually you stick it in your pocket and forget about it.

Joe was a great mechanic—twenty years ago. He could tune an engine like nobody's business. People would come to him with some kerplunk in the carburetor, and he'd know just how to fix it. But Joe stopped learning, and cars started changing. They're all computerized now, with fuel injection and automatic everything. Heck, lots of cars don't even *have* carburetors anymore. So if your Pinto has broken down, go see Joe. But if your car was built since 1980, he really can't help you.

Too many spouses are like Joe. They're experts in how their mates used to be, but they haven't kept up with the changes. Joe needs to enroll in some continuing education courses, and so do most spouses. They need to study up on the latest developments in their partner's wishes, interests, wants, and dreams.

## THE ALPHABET OF MARRIAGE

I'm tempted to say that need-meeting in a marriage is "as easy as A-B-C." But it's not. It can be pretty difficult sometimes. But I've come up with a few simple points to help you along—you might call them the "ABC's" of marriage, with a D thrown in (for "Difficult"?).

### FOR WOMEN

#### Assertively Participate in Sex

Remember that sexual fulfillment is probably a major need of your husband. (Ask him.) Meeting this need means more than just putting up with his sexual advances; it means having fun with him in the process, coming up with creative ways to share your sexuality.

One woman at a seminar told me how, at the urging of her girlfriends, she went to meet her husband at the airport after a business trip. Though she wasn't an exhibitionist at all, she wanted to excite her husband, so she wore a trench coat and basically nothing else. It was a great plan—until the metal detector went off.

The security guard couldn't understand why she refused to take off her coat, but they finally determined it was the belt of the coat that set off the alarm, and they let her through. She won't be trying that again anytime soon.

Harrowing as it was, this woman's effort to "aggressively participate in sex" was greatly appreciated by her husband. You don't have to go quite that far, but what *can* you do? What would your husband like? I've heard women say, "That's not the way I am." But a lot of things you want your husband to do don't come naturally to him either. The question is simply: Do you really want to please your husband?

### Become Interested in Your Sex Life

I remember seeing a cartoon with two birds on a branch, one of them looking amorous. The other says, "I know we're lovebirds, but I still have a headache."

Different attitudes toward sex have caused problems in many marriages. I'm reminded of an advice column where a woman wrote in saying she wanted to forget about having sex with her husband entirely, after thirty years of marriage. She had paid her dues, done her duty, fulfilled her marital responsibilities, and was just going through the motions to please her husband. In the following weeks, thousands of women wrote in to agree.

I was glad to see one of my favorite columnists, Jim Sanderson, publish a male response. "You cannot believe the frustration and ultimately the anger a man feels in trying to excite and express his love to a woman who, month after month, year after year, is only paying her dues. Quite often her passive resistance finally defeats him. He forgets the joy and strength he once knew. She emasculates him."

Men not only need sexual fulfillment, they need to be needed. And when they feel needed *sexually*, that's the best. If you really want to please your husband, don't just go through the motions. Learn about your own sexuality and enjoy it. Take the time to teach him how to please you, so you can share this God-given gift together.

### Creatively Please Him

Don't let me tell you what your husband needs. I don't know your husband. I can speak in terms of generalities—"most men"—but I can't give you the specifics of your relationship. You have to ask him. He may not even tell you right away, but keep asking. Find out what he needs and then do everything you can to meet those needs.

Break out of your own comfort zones and find creative ways to meet his needs. Try some things you've never done before. My wife, as I've indicated, is a very private person. Sexually, she observes what I call the Half-Mile Rule: We can't be together sexually if there's anyone within a half-mile. If a neighbor's garage door opens, she shuts down. The moment a car flicks its turn signal on the next street over, she's worried that someone will hear us. Me, a dump truck could drive into the bedroom and I wouldn't care. Yes, we're very different, but I'm grateful that Sande has broken out of some of her comfort zones in trying to please me.

### Develop Companionship

Never stop dating. Go along with your husband on the activities he enjoys. It's great if you learn to like the sports he likes, but that's not necessary. Just be there.

When we were dating, Sande told me she loved to fish. Later I realized *I* was the fish. When I'd take her on a fishing trip, she'd lie down on the boat. I mentioned this to a professor of mine, and I'll never forget his wise words: "As a couple you can do different things together."

### FOR MEN

### Ask Her Opinion

I asked speaker and author James Dobson for one piece of advice about marriage. I really appreciated what he said: "Before you do anything in life, run it by Sande first." I've

161

tried to do that—most of this book has benefited from her critical eye. And I pass that on to you. Get in the habit of asking your wife's opinion.

"But she doesn't understand what I'm dealing with!" you might say. You'd be surprised how much she does understand. And even if she doesn't grasp all the details, she may give you a valuable perspective. Women in general are closer to life than men are. We should learn to seek their wisdom.

### Become Conversational and Open

This will be painful, but grit your teeth and do it. Try to get past the surface levels of communication. Start some sentences with the words "I feel." If that's too tough, then create a word picture. "Sometimes I just feel like I'm a piece of balsa wood floating on the big, wide ocean." Or something like that. It doesn't have to be Shakespeare, just say how you feel—not just what you think.

### Commit to Listening to Her

Sande says I don't listen. I'm not sure why. So I sometimes show up at the wrong restaurant when I'm supposed to meet her for dinner. That could happen to anyone!

Seriously, a lot of guys have this problem. We start listening to our wives but then we tune out because we're not getting any important new information. Or so we think. But learn to read *how* your wife is saying things, not just *what* she's saying. Hear the facts, but also the feelings. Try not to think about what to say in response. Ask questions to clarify what she has said. Be sure you get it. She'll love you for that.

### Discover Her Love Language

The next chapter will deal fully with the five "love languages"—the specific ways we show love and want to receive love. If you're not showing love the right way, she may not be getting it.

# 8

## "Dr. Leman, You're Overdrawn"

**H**ave you ever bounced a check? I have. Not intentionally, mind you. I just thought I made a deposit in my checking account that was greater than it really was. It was really just a misunderstanding between my bank and me. Hey, what's an extra zero among friends?

Of course the bank didn't see it my way, and the bank won. I had to hurry to transfer some funds from my business account and send a new check to my creditor. With bank fees and penalties at $25 a pop, that little misunderstanding cost me a few bucks.

The same kind of misunderstanding can cost you dearly in your marriage.

My friend Willard Harley came up with the term "the Love Bank"[5] to describe the way husbands and wives balance their relationship. It's a helpful concept. Basically, Dr. Harley says that we all have "love bank" accounts in which we are either making deposits or withdrawals all day long as we interact with people. For example, suppose the husband comes home from work to find his wife frazzled and emotional after a difficult day. Instead of asking her, "What's for dinner?" he takes her hand, leads her into the den, and sits on the sofa with her, putting his arm around her and asking her to share with him the things that are on her mind. Then he says, "Honey, I'm sorry you've had such a hard day. . . . Listen, I don't want you to worry about fixing dinner. Why don't we go out to a nice restaurant?"

That husband has made a substantial deposit in his love bank account.

But then suppose if, in the same situation, the husband comes home and says to his wife, "For crying out loud, what's wrong with you?"

"Well, it was a rough day."

"Rough day? What do you know about having a rough day? It's not like you have that much to do around here anyway. . . . And, speaking of things you have to do, haven't you even started dinner yet?"

Obviously, that husband has made a hefty withdrawal from his love bank account. In fact, he may have just about emptied the account.

Harley says that in everything we do, we are either making deposits or withdrawals in our love banks, and urges that we always be trying to build up those accounts, just as we would be interested in building our own personal savings accounts.

Sometimes couples make so many withdrawals from each other's account that the love bank is empty. They have no feeling left for each other. When the husband needs support from the wife, it's not there because he hasn't made any deposits for a long time. When the wife needs the husband to listen compassionately, he doesn't because she hasn't done much for him lately. Both of them are "bouncing checks" like crazy.

This is a tragic situation, and I trust you're not there yet. You're probably trying to keep some kind of balance in your love bank accounts, supporting each other (making deposits) and drawing support from each other (making withdrawals).

The problem for you is probably one of communication. Your "bank statements" may not always reconcile. In fact, if you're like me, you have a hard time even understanding your bank statements. You see, you get love bank statements from your spouse all the time, except they're invisible.

"Is anything wrong, honey?"

"No."

"Are you sure there's nothing wrong?"

"I SAID THERE IS NOTHING WRONG!"

Now you just got a bank statement in that little exchange, but do you have any idea what it said? Because of these problems of interpretation, you may think you made a hefty deposit in your spouse's love bank when your spouse considered it insignificant. Just as I overestimated the amount I put into my bank account, and suffered the consequences, you may be overestimating the importance of what you're doing for your spouse.

Joe has no qualms about sprawling on the couch to watch football and calling out, "Honey, could you bring me some chips?" He's making a withdrawal from his wife's love bank, but he thinks he can afford it because he helped with the dishes. But "helping with the dishes" amounted to running a towel over three glasses and letting the rest air-dry. When his wife drop-kicks the bag of Doritos into the TV, he wonders what's going on. The truth is, his check just bounced. He thought he'd made a deposit, but his bank statement didn't line up with hers. The irony here is that this man, now adorned in his baggy boxers and T-shirt, with maybe a little extra belly to boot, used to bring her a single rose, complete with a little love note. Meanwhile, she's wondering, "Whatever happened to the man I married?"

I don't know about you, but these automatic teller machines get me in trouble. I know I should hang on to my receipts, but usually I lose them and rarely remember to record the withdrawals. And these "minor" withdrawals can add up. When I check my bank statement, I'm amazed at how often I've used the ATM and how little I have left in my account. Talk about shock therapy!

You're way ahead of me, aren't you? You've already guessed that the same thing happens in marriage. Every day you make minor withdrawals from your account in your spouse's love bank. An insensitive comment, a favor you ask, an outburst of emotion. You may think you're withdrawing just a little each time, but these things add up. If you're not replenishing your account on a regular basis, you'll be in trouble.

Sometimes you don't even know about the withdrawal. Your spouse looks for you and you're not there—you lose a point, *even though you're not there!* Your spouse misunderstands something you say, takes it as an insult—you lose two points, *even though you didn't mean it!* Your spouse can blame you for things you have nothing to do with, and you lose points in your account, whether you deserve it or not.

I never said marriage was easy, and often marriage isn't fair, but you can save yourself a lot of grief if you simply reconcile your love bank statements on a regular basis. Do you balance your checkbook? Do you go through the bank statements to make sure your records match theirs? Well, it's the same with your love bank—and your spouse is the banker. You've got to talk about where each of you gained points and lost points.

## SPEAKING THE SAME LANGUAGE

Why do we have such trouble reconciling our love bank statements? Because we're not always speaking the same language.

Gary Chapman has done some brilliant work in this area of "love languages." People express their love, he says, in different ways. And they expect to receive love in that same way. If you're not offering your love in your spouse's love language, the love isn't getting through. If that's the case, no wonder your love bank statements don't match! One bank is counting rubles and the other is counting yen. They're not going to come up with the same totals.

So let me summarize Chapman's five love languages and show how they can affect your love bank deposits and withdrawals.

### WORDS OF AFFIRMATION

Some people excel at paying sincere compliments and offering encouraging words to those they love. Others don't. But those who know this love language always seem to have something nice to say, and they often expect kind words in return. They comment on their spouses' appearance, talents, achievements, or attitude, but they can feel neglected when they don't hear similar affirming words from their mates.

One hallmark of this love language is the way people ask for what they want. "Love makes requests, not demands," writes Chapman.[6] That requires humility. Demands are put-downs, implying, "I'm important and you're not. Do this for me. Your desires don't matter." On the other hand, a humble request gives the other person a choice: "You probably have more important things to do, but would you consider doing this for me? I'd be grateful."

Words of affirmation aren't my specialty. My family still kids me about one time we all went out to eat at a lovely restaurant overlooking Lake Chautauqua in New York. "Table for seven," I requested.

"Seven?" the hostess repeated, looking at me as if I had a screw loose. You'd have thought I was asking her to seat seven thousand. For some reason, restaurants find it hard to accommodate a family with more than two children.

Anyway, the place must have been fairly busy, because they couldn't find a place for us in their main dining room. Eventually they shunted us off to a kind of sun porch, an ugly, dreary room if there ever was one. I felt like we were being sent to the barn while everyone else ate in the palace.

I stopped, formed a T with my hands, and said, "Whoa! Time out! Excu-u-se me, but we aren't sitting in here." No words of affirmation here: I sounded like a snippy little brat not getting my way. Oh, we did get another table, but I also alienated the hostess and embarrassed my family. (Of course, they've continued to tease me about this: "Whoa! Time out! Excu-u-se me!") Would it have been any harder to say nicely, "Do you think we could have a table in the dining room?"

Maybe I learned my lesson. On another occasion I was trying to get myself interviewed on a particular syndicated TV show. My publicist had sent the producer my promotional material, but the show just didn't want me. So I took matters into my own hands and called the producer myself.

That's a no-no in the media business, I've learned. Publicists and agents make the calls, not the guests. But I wanted to stir things up a little, and I really wanted to get on that show. When the producer's secretary answered the phone, however, I tried a tactic of affirmation rather than demand.

"Could you help me?" I asked. And at that point she had little choice but to say yes. I was identifying myself as someone who needed help and her as someone who had the power to help me. That's affirming.

"How can I help you?" she offered, and I said I wanted to speak with the producer. Of course, she asked who was calling.

"Mr. Nobody," I replied.

"Pardon me?"

"Mr. Nobody," I repeated. "That's N-O-B-O-D-Y."

She asked me again, and I said, "Well, I have a name— Kevin Leman—but trust me, I'm really a nobody. Yet I'd really like to talk to this producer for just a minute."

This woman had power, and I was affirming that. If I had ranted and raved about how important I was and how she had *better* put me through to her boss if she knew what was good for her—I'd be hearing a dial tone within a nanosecond. But I humbled myself and made a nice request, and I did get through to the producer and talked him into doing a show with me.

That's the power of affirmation.

The people who use this love language tend to be verbal, at ease with words. They express themselves well. Sure, there are some verbal people who use words as weapons, delighting in the development of biting insults. But those who use words of affirmation find joy in using language to uplift others.

Yet when they overdo it, misunderstandings can occur. If compliments seem insincere, they don't mean much. And nonverbal people don't trust words as much as verbal people do. They can read insincerity or sarcasm into all sorts of innocent comments. So if a verbal person who uses words of affirmation as a love language is married to a nonverbal person who uses one of the other love languages, there can be a discrepancy between their love banks.

Let's say Perry uses this verbal love language and Sherry doesn't. "You look lovely tonight," he says after dinner.

169

"I really like your hair like that. I've been thinking about you all day. You're the most beautiful woman in the world."

And she's thinking, "Yeah, right! Thank you, but I know I'm no Cindy Crawford. You're probably just saying all this to get me into bed."

So when bedtime comes, Perry's amorous and Sherry's arctic. He wonders why she's not returning his kisses. After all, he deposited those four compliments after dinner (and probably many more since then). He should have at least four credits in his account, right?

But in Sherry's accounting method, those compliments didn't count for much. He gets maybe half a credit for trying, but she didn't really believe any of them. She wishes he would have shown his love by running out to the store for some supplies she said she needed, or by sitting with her in the TV room rather than working at his computer.

Those are examples of other love languages. If Perry had learned to use those love languages to express his love, he would be making major deposits in Sherry's love bank, and she would almost certainly be more receptive to his amorous advances.

### QUALITY TIME

Other people show their love by simply *being there,* by spending time with their mates. I should say it's a matter of being *completely* there, being a companion, not just taking up space. As Chapman says, "Quality time does not mean that we have to spend our together moments gazing into each other's eyes. It means that we are doing something together and that we are giving our full attention to the other person."[7]

In the love language of quality time, people love doing things together—going on trips, going out to dinner, rollerblading, backpacking, or shopping. Willard Harley calls it "recreational companionship," doing the things you love to do with the person you love to do them with. It's *dating*, when you think about it. What's dating, really, except spending time together to get to know each other. *What* you do is secondary, as long as you're doing it together. A lot of couples have forgotten how to date. With today's busy schedules, husbands and wives hurry past each other like minivans on the interstate. Some can function like this. But if one of the partners has the love language of quality time, they'd better stop passing each other.

Believe it or not, I'm a quality time person. Any time I can get alone with Sande, I'm a happy dude. The trouble is, those moments don't happen enough. If I want quality time with her, with all that goes on in my house, I have to go to the master bedroom and bolt and lock the door in four places. Sometimes you have to fight for your quality time.

Chapman talks about different "dialects" in these love languages. Simple *togetherness* is one dialect of the quality time love language; *quality conversation* is another. Nonverbal people just love to hang out together; verbal people need to talk.

Of course, quality conversation is more than a weather report. It requires involvement, eye contact, full attention—what the experts call *active listening*. You need to listen through the words for the feelings being expressed. You need to understand the body language. Quality conversation has a fair amount of silence woven in, but not much interruption. It's a soul-to-soul connection, not just mind-to-mind.

Now what happens if Kim has the love language of quality time and Tim has the love language of words of affirmation? Tim kisses Kim on the way out the door, saying, "You are so wonderful to me. I wish I could stay, but I've got that board meeting. Thanks for understanding. I love you." And he's gone.

Tim thinks he deposited some credits in his love bank account with those loving words. He doesn't realize he's making withdrawals with every hour he's not home. Every time Kim sees something funny on TV, she thinks, "I'll have to remember to tell Tim about that. But of course he's not here, because the board meeting's more important than I am." *Ka-ching.* More taken out of the till.

Then Tim comes home, lavishing more words of affirmation on his wife. She wants to know everything about the meeting; that's her way of sharing the experience with him. But he's tired. He doesn't want to go through that again. When it's obvious he doesn't want to talk, she shares her experience of watching TV, talking with her mom on the phone, reading a Gothic romance.

This all gets a bit wearisome for Tim, who's already had his fill of conversation for the evening. He's thinking, "Why didn't she bother to ask whether I wanted to hear about her phone conversation? In all her chatter, she hasn't offered a word of appreciation for all the work I do to support this family. She doesn't care that I'm all worn out."

In Kim's love language, this quality conversation would be scoring big points. But all Tim needs are a few words of affirmation, and he's not getting any. So her account is depleted as well.

### GIFTS

Still other people communicate their love in the language of gift-giving. And they look to receive love from others in the same way. "Gifts are visual symbols of love," says Chapman.[8] This isn't a matter of money. A wildflower picked from the roadside can mean as much as a diamond bracelet. It's more a matter of involvement, of interest, of care. My gift to you is a token of my feelings for you. I invest a certain amount of emotion, wisdom, time, expense, and effort in the process of imagining, creating, choosing, buying, wrapping, or transporting a gift to you—all because I love you.

Certain types of people gravitate to this love language. They tend to be artistic but down-to-earth. Their homes are filled with mementos—a drawing on a refrigerator door, a vase from dear Aunt Edna, a trophy from high school. Each of the objects has meaning. Each item carries love.

Please don't think of these people as greedy. Sure, they like the objects they're given, but they really prize the love behind them. The gifts are physical evidence of the love involved.

I am married to a world-class gift-giver. Sande *invents* reasons to give gifts to people, and they're always impeccably wrapped. The night before we're having friends over for dinner, she'll be baking little heart-shaped cookies to place in party favors that our guests can take home. I don't have the same gift-giving nature. I figure we're already giving them dinner, why can't *I* eat the cookies?

Seriously, I'm a little bit bothered that she's baking for our friends instead of coming to bed with me. But I've had to learn to respect her gift-giving nature, even though I don't share it. I've also learned that she loves to *receive* meaningful gifts, which means I have to give them.

Guys, never give your wife a toaster. I'm telling you from experience. And wives, don't give your husband a weed-whacker, unless he specifically asks for one. Gifts like that just say, "Get to work." They don't communicate love. Good gift-giving requires that we look "behind our spouses' eyes" to see what they want and need.

Serious misunderstandings can arise in homes like mine, with one spouse who has the love language of gifts and another who doesn't. Unless you regularly balance your love bank statements, you can get into trouble.

Say Dan wants to get his wife Jan a particular necklace for her birthday. He chases through three counties to find a store with just the right one. When he finally finds it, he's excited. All of the searching was worth it, because he wants to show his deep love for her with this extravagant gift. The thing is, they've invited friends over for dinner. With all the chasing around, Dan gets home about two minutes before the guests arrive. Jan is hustling about the kitchen when Dan bursts in, and she gives him an icy glare. He's all hugs and kisses: "Sorry, I'm late, but I have a great reason. Wait till you see it."

Though he planned to give her the gift later, he figures he has to do something to cheer her up, so he gleefully places the nicely wrapped gift on the kitchen counter.

"What's that?" she asks, eyeing the gift skeptically.

"Open it."

"I've got to get ready."

"Open it!"

"I can't!" she protests. "The place is still a mess. I've had to do all this myself."

"I know," he coos. "But open it, please. I went to a lot of trouble for this."

"Later," she says, and goes to find the vacuum cleaner.

All through dinner they put on their best faces for the company's sake, but they're both hurting inside. Dan wants credit for working so hard to find this gift, which Jan won't even open. Obviously Dan's love language is gift-giving. But Jan is more fluent in our next love language, acts of service. She is peeved that Dan left her alone to prepare dinner for guests *on her own birthday*. And he said he'd be home early to help, no later than 4 P.M.

So Dan expects his love bank account to be full, since he put in several hours of hard labor at shopping for the perfect gift. In reality it's empty, because he wasn't home helping out. Jan expects Dan to appreciate the fact that she pulled off this dinner by herself, but he's hurt because she didn't show appreciation for his gift. So her account in his love bank is deceptively low too.

## ACTS OF SERVICE

We got a peek at this love language with Dan and Jan. Many people, like Jan, see love in terms of *doing things for others.* That's how they show love, and that's how they expect love to be shown to them.

I think of that song in *Fiddler on the Roof,* where Tevye asks his wife, Golde, "Do you love me?" She responds, "For twenty-five years I've washed your clothes, cooked your meals, cleaned your house, given you children, milked the cow." For a quarter-century she had offered him acts of service. As she sings later, "If that's not love, what is?"

But many misunderstandings can occur even within this love language. Couples don't always agree on the division of labor within the home. For example, who takes out the trash? His mom always did it when he was growing up, so he expects his wife to do it. But in her home it was Dad's job, so she waits for her husband to do it. Unless they reach some agreement, this house will get pretty smelly.

In any home there are expectations and extras. It's nice when we get appreciation for doing our normal chores, but we don't need it. We're just expected to do those things. It's the *extra* acts of service that we do for love, for which we expect extra love in return.

She may always prepare dinner, but tonight she makes his favorite dessert. That's extra.

He may always clean the bathroom, but today he cleans the kitchen too, so she doesn't have to. That's extra.

She washes his car. He makes her breakfast in bed. He's sick as a dog, so she waits on him hand and foot for three days. She's headed off on a business trip and busy with last-

175

minute preparations, so he types up her business report. These aren't normal chores, they're extras. And this is how many husbands and wives show their love.

But not all of them.

A lot of men are service-challenged. I'm generalizing, of course. Some women have this malady too, and I know a number of men who are great servants, but I think we still have a culture where women do two-thirds of the work. Many wives are bringing home the bacon and cooking it too. Men will mow the lawn and keep the vehicles running. They may even keep their sports gear in order and make sure the TV is in working order. (Me, I'm still trying to figure out how to keep the VCR from blinking 12:00, 12:00, 12:00.) But most of the work in the house is done by women.

And if that's the way you both want it, no problem. But it can create problems when the wife uses the acts of service love language and the husband doesn't.

After dinner, Will kisses Jill and says, "Great meal, honey. You're such a good cook."

"Thanks, Will," she replies. "But I've got a ton of stuff to do before that meeting tonight. I have to wash the dishes, make the sandwiches for tomorrow, call Carol and Kathy about Saturday, and help Tyler learn his lines for the school play."

"When's the meeting?" he asks, as any sensitive man would.

"In a half hour," she says, already running water for the dishes.

"I guess you have your work cut out for you. But you'll do it. I know you can," he says caringly. "I'll be out working on the car."

And he leaves her with a ton of stuff to do.

What love language was Will using? Words of affirmation. He was very encouraging to his overworked wife. But

Jill was using the acts of service love language, serving her husband, her child, and her community. She is a little miffed that he isn't pitching in to help. He may be bothered later that she doesn't show any appreciation for the work he put into polishing the car. He wants affirming words, which he doesn't get.

Do they love each other? Absolutely. They just have different ways of showing it. Unfortunately, Jill may think she's making deposits in Will's love bank for all her acts of service, when he's really taking most of them for granted. In fact, he's deducting from her account when he doesn't get the affirming words he needs. Of course he thinks his account balance is high in her love bank because of all his kind words, but he's making withdrawals every time he doesn't pitch in to help around the house.

### Physical Touch

The final love language is one I know well: physical touch. Ask my wife. I am a toucher, and I love to be a touchee. Let me confess it here: I am a reformed grabber. That's how I show love and how I like to receive it.

Not long ago, I got home from work and was greeted by my twelve-year-old, Hannah. "Do you want to hear some more bad news?" she asked. I already knew an upstairs toilet had malfunctioned, necessitating a call to the plumber and a major cleanup in the bathroom. Now Hannah was telling me the sewage had seeped downstairs, into a closet, ruining some clothes and toys and carpets.

Obviously Sande had been having a bad day. But finally, later that night, the plumber was gone, the carpets were up, the fans were blowing. The house still smelled pretty bad, but we could finally relax a little. Sande grabbed her nightly cup of coffee and vegged out in the easy chair.

A half hour later, I sauntered into the room and said, as only a husband can say to a wife, "You wanna fool around?" I had this Bullwinkle-the-moose look on my face—how could she resist me?

Well, Sande's eyes popped open and she managed a wry smile. "Do I look like I want to fool around?"

I'm the expert, right? I've got books and seminars and tapes and a TV show, telling everyone else about marriage. How could I be so insensitive to my wife's frame of mind? Well, it comes naturally. I was in the mood for some physical touch, and I wasn't about to let a little sewage disaster stop me.

You should know by now that by "physical touch" I'm not just talking about sex, though sexual intimacy is part of this. I'm talking about little kisses as well as big kisses, about hand-holding as well as fondling, about bear hugs, backrubs, an arm around the shoulder, and playing footsie. I'm talking about sharing the armrest at a movie theater and lightly stroking her hand. Some people, like me, need this kind of loving. Others seem totally immune to it.

Let's say Alice is married to, uh, Dallas. And he hasn't touched her for six months. Naturally, Alice wonders if she's unattractive to him. The fact is, he's just not a touch kind of guy. If she doesn't initiate physical contact, it doesn't happen. A month ago she got tired of initiating it. So now it doesn't happen.

Other than that, Dallas is the best husband in the world. He's always doing things for Alice, making sure she's happy. He does a lot of the housework, especially now that Alice is working so much. He'll get up at 3 A.M. and drive across town to get her some cough syrup, without even being asked. That's just the kind of guy he is. But he's not a toucher.

Meanwhile, Dallas is unhappy in this relationship too. He feels he's doing all the work—especially in the last month or so. Alice started working later and is quite tired when she gets home. Dallas doesn't mind waiting on her, but he thinks the marriage is out of balance. He wonders if she started having an affair.

You guessed it. Alice's love language is physical touch. Dallas's is acts of service. Both are giving love in their own ways and frustrated because they're not receiving it in those ways. Both of them think their love bank accounts should be overflowing, but both are really scraping bottom.

Physical touch is often something we learn from our families, and Dallas's problem with touch may be a result of a certain aloofness he felt growing up. Alice thought she was marrying one man, but she ended up with his whole family, in a way. In fact, she might be paying for the sins of her mother-in-law in this relationship. If his mom was either distant or smothering, Dallas might have learned to avoid touching the women in his life.

On the other hand, Alice probably comes from a huggy family, one in which love was expressed through affectionate, non-threatening touch. Our families of origin affect us positively as well as negatively.

In any case, Alice and Dallas find themselves sending their love right past each other. Neither one is hearing their own love language, so both feel unloved—even though they're both trying very hard to show love in the only way they know how.

## SO, WHAT?

The solution for all of our mismatched couples sounds simple: Learn your spouse's love language and use it. There's no shortage of love here, but their love banks aren't making the proper transfers. Their "bank statements" aren't reconciling.

I know it's no fun to sit down each month with your checkbook (or increasingly, your computer) and balance it with the bank's report. But it's something you have to do to maintain a healthy bank account. It's the same thing in marriage. You have to sit down together regularly to discuss the balances in your love bank accounts. How are you doing? How am I doing? Are you receiving the love I'm sending? Do I need to try harder to speak your language?

## Action, Not Words

### 1. Discover your partner's love language and your own.

This isn't too complicated. What does your spouse complain about? What bothers you most about the kind of love you're *not* getting from your spouse? Or, on the positive side, what expressions of love mean the most to you and your spouse? When have you felt the greatest love between you—how was it being shown?

You could make a game of this. Each of you take a paper and make two columns—His and Hers. Then go through the five love languages and each of you put one or two in each column, whichever love languages you think are "spoken" by you and your spouse (many people have two or more). Then compare notes. You'll probably be pretty close. It's surprising how obvious this is once you start thinking about it.

### 2. Attempt to show love in your spouse's language.

This won't be easy at first if you don't share the same love language. But it's all part of "getting behind the eyes" of your spouse. Be creative in finding ways to communicate love in your *spouse's* language, not your own.

If your spouse appreciates words of affirmation, then work on those words. Write a love poem, send a card with your thoughts of love, take a moment to say how much you love him or her. If it's quality time, get out your datebook and schedule some outings together, or just reserve some quiet evenings at home. If gifts are needed, start researching the kind of gifts your spouse would appreciate most. If your spouse loves acts of service, list the things you could do—including some special items like breakfast in bed. If it's physical touch, well, I'm sure you can think of something.

If you're having trouble thinking of something, ask your spouse to name the nicest thing you ever did for him or her. Might not be a bad idea to try that again.

You can make this a game too. Brainstorm the possibilities and come up with a list of twenty, if you can. Then rank them, or have your spouse rank them, and do one a week for the next month (at least).

### 3. COACH YOUR SPOUSE IN USING YOUR LOVE LANGUAGE.

If you were to move to France, it would take a while for you to pick up the language. The same is true of love languages. Don't demand too much too soon. They take a while to speak fluently.

Along the way, you'll need to be a tutor, teaching your spouse how you like to be loved. Be careful about nagging, show appreciation for the effort, and be honest about what works and what doesn't.

I heard one woman complaining, "I've got five kids and a Suburban packed with groceries. I'm lugging in bag after bag, and my husband just sits there in his easy chair, reading the paper, and he will not get up and help unless I ask him. It makes me so mad! I don't want to ask him, because he should know!"

Sure, he should know. But apparently acts of service is not his love language. This wife may need to do some remedial training to help him love her effectively.

### 4. TALK REGULARLY ABOUT YOUR LOVE BANK BALANCES.

Don't get caught by surprise with a low love bank balance. Keep talking about where you stand. And *listen!* Don't be planning your response when your spouse is giving you important information. Talk one at a time, and repeat what you hear until you're sure you understand. Then pray about it, asking to be more perceptive.

I know it's hard to say to your spouse, "Hey, you need to love me better!" But that's why these terms and analogies are so helpful. The love bank. Love languages. These are ways that you can start talking about the love you need and the love you're offering. It gives us a vocabulary to use in this subject of love, a subject we all need to learn a lot more about.

# 9

## How to Be Good and Angry

A few weeks ago, I had to run by Kmart on my way home from the office to pick up a couple of things.

I paid for my purchases and headed to my car, just behind a woman pushing a shopping cart full of her purchases, and a boy of perhaps seven or eight. Now I have no idea what the boy had done—I didn't see him do anything wrong—but the woman, who I assume was his mother, was terribly angry.

"I don't know why you do such stupid things," she said. "You make me so angry. I just hate to take you anywhere."

The boy didn't say anything. He just trudged along beside her, but the slump in his shoulders said that he heard every word.

And still, Mom wasn't through.

"I don't know why you have to mess up everything. You're just a . . . disgrace."

The woman's tirade continued as they reached their car and she began to unload her shopping cart into the backseat. By now, they were so far away from me that I could no longer hear what she was saying, but I could still detect the sharp and angry tone in her voice. You know the old saying, "Sticks and stones may break my bones, but names will never hurt me," but I was quite sure that each one of her angry words was hitting the boy with the same force as a good-sized stone. But still, he didn't even raise a whimper in protest. He simply soaked it all in as if he deserved every bit of it.

I sat in my car for a moment, debating whether to go over and talk to the woman. I don't like to butt in other people's affairs unless I am asked, but I was beginning to think that this might be a good time to make an exception. By now the woman and boy were in their car and pulling out of the parking lot. I had hesitated a moment too long. But as I watched them go, I breathed a quick prayer that the woman would quit reacting to the child in this way, and that the boy would know he did not deserve this kind of treatment.

What was wrong with this situation? Did the woman have a right to be angry? As I said, I have no idea what the boy did, but let's assume he did something "terrible," such as overturning a big display in the middle of the store and that his mother had every right in the world to be angry with him.

What was wrong was that she had no idea how to handle or control her anger. She was letting it pour out of her in ways that were destructive to the boy and to her role as his parent.

What's more, she was focusing her anger directly onto the boy instead of on whatever it was he had done that had caused her so much trouble. She was telling him that *he* was a disgrace, that she hated to go anywhere with *him,* and that *he* was stupid.

She hadn't learned the importance and effectiveness of focusing anger on the *act,* rather than the *person* committing the act.

Whatever was going on, this mother had the right to be angry. Absolutely. So do you. Sometimes you have the right to become angry because of something one of your children has done. Sometimes you have the right to become angry because of something your spouse, or other loved one, has done. But having the right to be angry is not the same as having the right to lash out in retaliation at those who have angered you or to seek to hurt them.

"But, Dr. Leman," someone asks, "don't I have the right to express my anger?"

Yes, of course, as long as you express it in ways that are not destructive and that will ultimately strengthen, rather than destroy, the other person and your relationship with him or her.

If I get angry with my wife and tell her that she's stupid, and that she's always messing things up, then she's not likely to be in much of a loving mood toward me. But if, on the other hand, I am able to say, "I really get angry when such and such happens," then I've helped to diffuse the situation. I haven't said, "It's your fault," but rather, "I get angry." From that starting point, we can discuss whether my anger is justified. Perhaps it is, and if so, then the person who has caused it, if she loves me, will apologize and resolve never again to do what makes me so angry. Or perhaps I am angry because I have misunderstood the situation, and if so, then a careful explanation of things should serve to alleviate my anger. A third possibility is that there is really no justification for my anger at all, and that I am simply being unreasonable. In this instance, I'll feel a lot better later on, when I come to my senses, knowing that I didn't stomp around and bluster and accuse others when the situation was really my own fault.

Again, a key is whether we express anger toward the act or the individual. For instance, a father can say, "I am really angry that this milk shake is spilled all over the car seat, but I can get a rag and clean it up." This way he is not denying the fact of his anger but is finding a satisfactory solution to his feelings—which is cleaning it up. Or enlisting the help of the one who spilled the milk shake to get the mess cleaned up. In this situation, Dad's three-year-old daughter, who just made the colossal mess, will not be made to feel guilty. His anger is directed toward the "goop" and not toward his little girl.

Once he's finished cleaning up the mess, Dad can urge his daughter to be more careful in the future, but he can do it in a loving and gentle way, without that nasty edge in his voice.

Most of us have never really dealt with anger. We have been taught to turn it inward, toward ourselves, keeping our real feelings inside. Then, in pressure-cooker fashion, the hurts, feelings, and frustrations begin to boil to the surface. We "blow" and our anger becomes destructive because it lashes out at anyone who is unfortunate enough to be in the way. Too often, the recipients of this anger are the ones we love the most.

I find in counseling married couples that anger is often accentuated after the bedroom door closes. For example, Nadine complained to me that every time she turned around, her husband, Bob, was getting "frisky." The couple was in their forties, and even though Nadine said she enjoyed sex as much as anyone, "We're not a couple of newlyweds."

Bob defended himself by saying that he couldn't help it if he had a strong sex drive. Moreover, he made his wife feel guilty for not always being submissive to him or ready to "party" whenever he was in the mood. The truth was that Bob was a very angry person who had never learned how to communicate with his wife on a satisfactory basis and who was afraid to tell her how insecure he really was. He controlled his feelings of inadequacy by his seemingly macho, aggressive, and insatiable sexual appetite.

For years Nadine avoided Bob, faked it, and invented excuses—but Bob's hunger for sex continued. In counseling Nadine, I told her that she was missing the boat. It wasn't so much the sex that Bob wanted from her as it was a continual reaffirmation of his dominance over her. He showed it sexually.

You should have seen the surprised look on Nadine's face when I suggested that she submit not only every time Bob approached her for sex, but that she also go the extra mile and initiate the act. In spite of her initial reluctance, she took my suggestion. As she began to chase after her husband, he became bewildered and unsure of their changing relationship. The more she pushed, the more he began to withdraw into a shell.

Within sixty days of applying this action-oriented method, Nadine's husband became impotent! Since Bob was no longer successful at dominating her in an aggressive manner, he turned to passive means (impotency) to do the same thing. (It's just as controlling to be impotent as it is to be overly aggressive.)

## FOUR RESPONSES TO ANGER

H. Norman Wright says that there are four basic responses to anger.[9]

He says that we either:

1. Suppress it
2. Express it
3. Repress it
4. Confess it

Let's take a closer look at these ways of dealing with anger.

### SUPPRESSED ANGER

Bob was an example of someone who suppressed his anger. He knew he was angry but he didn't know what to do about it. A person like this tries to keep his anger under wraps, hidden from the world. But eventually it has to spill out, and when it does it comes in uncontrolled actions or words. Bob's anger vented itself in controlling his wife. He manifested it by continually demanding sex from her.

When I was a boy, I used to love to shoot off firecrackers. (What boy doesn't?) Occasionally, though, I would throw one of them, and it would just sit there, with nothing happening.

"Well, that one was a dud," I'd say and then go over to see what the problem was. Usually, I was right. But once in a while I'd get a big surprise. That fuse would still be smoldering, and when I'd bend down to see why it had gone out—blam!!—that's when it would explode, right in my face. That's the way it is with a person who suppresses anger. He tries to present a calm exterior, but underneath it all he's smoldering away, and sooner or later he's going to explode.

### EXPRESSED ANGER

The person who expresses anger is the one who shows his well-developed temper. He is a controller and lets loose and tells by his action that he's ticked off and everybody better pay special attention to him. He may say, "I just naturally have a hot temper." But my counseling hasn't turned up any evidence that anyone is born with a naturally explosive temper.

Instead, my experience has been that when a person gains insight into his temper—and why he uses it the way he does—that temper usually dissipates into thin air. It often loses its purposeful nature once we have disclosed the psychological payoffs for the behavior. In essence, it lifts a heavy burden from the person when he can understand how he uses his temper in his relationships with others.

I had a surgeon as a client several years ago. In conversation in my office he appeared to be shy and withdrawn. It was only after I visited with his wife that I found out that this "shy person" punched holes in the walls of his house with his fists, and that he became terribly explosive whenever the tiniest thing went wrong. He was a controller, but while he was able to keep things "under control" in one area of his life, he wasn't able to do it in other areas.

Occasionally shyness can be a means of controlling a situation or of expressing anger. For example, notice a situation that occurs when several children come into a room for a party or activity of some type.

One of the children will invariably take a step backward and act as if he doesn't want to take part. Usually the adult in the room will make a special effort to go over and talk to little "Snooky" about joining the other children. The psychological dynamic of that situation is that the child is saying, "Hey! I'm very powerful. I don't come in like everyone else. I need a special invitation and an escort."

In going over and trying to induce the child to join the others in the activity, the adult is doing just the opposite of what he should be doing. The next time you're in a situation where a child chooses not to be in the group, let him stay out for a while. The natural consequence for not joining in will be that the child will miss out on a fun activity or something special, like ice cream and cake. Going over and giving special audience to the child is adding to his conviction that he counts in life only when he is in control of the situation.

189

## REPRESSED ANGER

Many times I see people in counseling sessions who have become depressed because they have bottled up and repressed their anger—their anger is buried deep within them. For example, I think of Carolyn, a genteel, Southern lady, who could never admit that she was angry because—I suppose—it just wasn't ladylike.

I don't know if she had ever been to charm school, but I suspect that she had, and I also suspect that the experience did her a tremendous amount of harm. She was all grace and charm and laughter on the outside, but underneath it all was a great deal of anger she had never dealt with.

Now she had a right to be angry. Her first husband had left her for one of her best friends, she had some physical problems, and she worked for an employer who did not appreciate her or treat her fairly.

And yet she would never admit that she was angry, or even that she had any *reason* to be angry.

"How could I be angry?" she'd ask. "God has done so much for me."

Every time we tried to talk about it, she would tell me how much God had given her.

I suppose she felt that it would be a sin to admit that she felt angry. And so she's still angry. And still telling everyone, including herself, that she isn't angry.

And she's also depressed but doesn't understand why, because "God has given her so much."

As I said, repression of anger will lead to depression, and although we think of depression in the negative sense, it is really productive behavior for the one who fears sharing his real self and real feelings with his mate. Depression may be used to get back at one's mate for perceived mistreatment. It may be a way of keeping someone over the proverbial barrel. Depression can be a crying out for someone to become involved and close. It can be a means of controlling the other person, as in, "How could you even think of doing something like that right now when you know how depressed I am?"

Lewis, a dentist, was a highly successful and respected person within the community. He was devoted to his work, a perfectionist (like most dentists) who had the innate capability of keeping people at arm's length. This meant that he could never open up to anyone—not even his wife—to share his emotions, including anger. His wife had started a business of her own and was gradually becoming financially and emotionally more independent. As she did so, his depression increased to such a degree that he could no longer function on a daily basis. What was happening was that he was repressing his anger.

Lewis had diagnosed himself as a chronic depressive and finally decided that psychotherapy might be of some assistance. As I listened to his tale of woe, I realized that his depression was probably purposive behavior. It was his way of telling his wife, "You can't leave me, particularly when I'm down." It was his final effort to keep her under control. When I disclosed to him the psychological, purposeful nature of his depression, it began to lift like a fog on a warm summer morning. Unfortunately, his repressed anger, his perfectionistic tendencies, and his need to keep people at arm's length were too deep-seated. He paid dearly for his inability to share his feelings, in that his wife grew tired of the relationship—in which she gave much and received very little in return—and finally went her own way.

### CONFESSED ANGER

The best way to handle anger is to confess it before it gets out of control or is tucked away—but be careful how you confess it. I remember a student in one of my counseling classes who told me that his wife made him angry. When I asked, "Now, Peter, where does the anger come from?" He said, "It comes from my wife." I told him that was impossible, because the anger can't pass from another person into you. You create, manufacture, and distribute your own anger.

Dr. David Augsburger suggests that when you find yourself using another person as a scapegoat you need to stop and "listen to yourself. Recognize what you're doing: avoiding responsibility; sidestepping the real problem; denying ownership of your feelings, responses, and actions. . . . My actions are mine. Your actions are yours. I am responsible for my behavior. You are responsible for yours."[10]

Of course, confessing anger in this way comes after you have answered the question, "Can I share it with my mate?" If we can get to the point where we can begin to share anger and frustration with each other in a positive way, that's when we are beginning to put together a marriage. If your boss has been on your back all day, don't go home and pick a fight with your mate.

Yes, in that situation, you are angry and in a bad mood. What usually happens is that you walk in the door grumbling like a grizzly bear that was rudely awakened right in the middle of his winter's nap.

Your spouse notices this right away and says something along the lines of, "Boy! Are you ever in a bad mood!"

And what do you say? "I am not!" And then you're even more grouchy and angry because you resent the fact that you've been accused of being in a bad mood, even though it's a 100 percent accurate accusation.

It would be better to confess your anger, to say something along the lines of, "You're right. I really am in a bad mood tonight. Let me tell you why I'm so angry." Then you can proceed to tell your spouse about the situation at work. In this way your spouse has become your ally in the situation; someone who can listen to you, sympathize with you, and help you deal with your feelings, instead of being someone who just happens to get in the way of your anger and gets steamrolled as a result.

David Augsburger, in his book *Be All You Can Be*, tells how you can make the most of your anger.

> Anger is a vital valid, natural emotion. As an emotion, it is in itself neither right nor wrong. The rightness or wrongness depends on the way it is released and exercised.
>
> Be angry, but be aware that anger quickly turns bitter, it sours into resentment, hatred, malice, and even violence unless it is controlled by love.
>
> Be angry, but only to be kind. Only when anger is motivated by love of your brother, by love of what is right for people, by what is called from you by the love for God, is it constructive, creative anger.
>
> Make the most of your anger. Turn it from selfish defensiveness to selfless compassion.[11]

How can you deal with anger? One way is to replace it with an act of love.

For example, suppose it's late on Saturday morning and your wife is still sound asleep. You've been puttering around the house, gradually making more and more noise because you think she ought to be up too. Suddenly, you make the decision that you're through with this business of being subtle. So you stomp into the bedroom and say, "You ought to be up! It's nearly ten o'clock! How long are you going to lie in that bed anyway?"

Needless to say, this is not going to get your weekend off to a very good start.

Now suppose you chose another approach. You went into the kitchen, made her a cup of coffee, brought it to her bedside, and began to rub her back softly. Yes, you're still angry. You're not really happy that she's still in bed, but the question is, do you love her? If you do, you'll put your own needs on the back burner for a while and see that she gets her needs met. Giving her a back rub and a cup of coffee when she awakens is going to make this a great Saturday for both of you. Everything is more effective when it's done in love rather than anger. Love really is a decision.

## USE YOUR ENERGY WISELY

The fact is that you have only so much energy to expend every day, and you have to decide how you are going to use it. In love? Or in anger? Doing for others? Or doing *to* others?

Some people live their lives as if they're out in the center of a big pool, treading water. They aren't making any progress in any direction. They're paddling like mad, but they're just not moving. That is the psychological plight of thousands of people. They don't go one way or the other; they just stay in the middle and feel safe. In this "safe" position they don't have to make the choices that life requires of them.

But the fact is that if you stay treading water long enough in life, you're going to drown. You cannot just tread water forever.

If there is something that needs to be done in your life today, begin to work toward doing it. The anxiety and anger will be made less by a decision to begin working on a solution to the problem, whatever the problem may be.

Maybe you've never learned to communicate your emotions. You've never been taught or never had the opportunity of sharing yourself with others. Perhaps your self-worth is so beaten down by your mate or your family that you have just thrown in the towel and given up. You feel that no one has ever tried or even wanted to meet your needs. If so, recognize the fact that it is all right to be angry. When you verbally express—confess—your anger, sharing it with someone else, you are really committing an act of love—if you feel anger toward the act, and not toward the person.

Begin to practice sharing with your mate now. Make a special time each day when the two of you can be together, and really talk about what's on your minds. You and your mate will not always be feeling good at the same time, but you can still be understanding of each other.

If you are indifferent to your mate's emotions, then you'd better check out your love clock and see if it's still ticking. Indifference breeds discontent, and discontent breeds danger.

## Action, Not Words

Whenever you and your spouse feel that there are some angry thoughts to be shared, it's a good idea to take a bath together. Does it sound crazy? Well, it works, so plunge in! Sit facing each other in the bathtub. This is probably the best environment within the home to discuss those angry feelings. After all, it's very difficult to get up, run to the next room, and close the door. This setting also removes all the barriers between you. But be sure to keep the rules in mind:

1. You have a right to be angry.
2. Anger should be directed at the act and not at the person.
3. Verbalize your anger.
4. Listen to the other person without thinking about what you are going to say in defense of yourself.

195

5. Be sure to be specific. No using vague generalities or sweeping exaggerations.
6. Ask your mate how he or she would like you to be different or how you can change your behavior.
7. Be sure to find a satisfactory solution to the anger.

# 10

## *Games Couples Play*

Let me ask you something: Who's winning your marriage?

What's your response to that question? Probably something like, "What do you mean, who's winning? Marriage isn't a competition—it's a partnership."

Well, yes, I know, but all the same I've noticed that many couples tend to approach it as if it were a track meet or a wrestling match. Instead of Prince and Princess Charming living happily ever after, their marriages resemble a three-falls match between Hulk Hogan and Vicious Victoria!

As a part of this competition, couples tend to play games with each other. Not nice, innocent, fun-loving games, but games that are designed to conquer the other spouse. More often than not, these games manifest themselves in the bedroom.

In this chapter I want to talk about a few of the more deadly games I've encountered from couples I've counseled in my private practice.

The first game I want to discuss is:

## KILL THE UMPIRE

Have you ever been to a baseball game and seen a play that nobody could quite figure out? One manager runs out of the dugout and argues that the play should be called his way, while the other manager comes out of his dugout just as quickly and argues just as vehemently that the call should go in his favor. Meanwhile the umpire pulls the rule book out of his hip pocket, and he feverishly tries to find the proper solution.

Of course, it doesn't matter what judgment he makes. One of those managers is going to wind up being very angry, and he's going to be on the umpire's case for the rest of the game—or at least until the ump gives him the old heave-ho and sends him to the showers.

Well, couples who play Kill the Umpire bring to their marriages a little book with all of the rules for life and marriage that they've been compiling for years. They know exactly what is expected in every situation, and if someone does something that goes against the rule book, well, there's going to be heck to pay.

If a couple is typical, for example, they have never received any premarital counseling about sex, and they haven't spent much time talking with each other about it either. So in trial-and-error fashion they go into the marital relationship and begin to explore. Now if the husband violates one of the rules in her little book, the wife is going to be like that umpire who won't put up with any nonsense from a belligerent manager.

"One more move like that, Charlie, and you're out of the game!"

My point is that we rarely share our personal rule books with our marriage partners. We don't talk to each other about certain things—especially about sex, because it's so, well . . . embarrassing. It's also one of the most important aspects of marriage, and it's well worth talking about—sharing likes, dislikes, and other feelings.

In my counseling sessions, I usually tell couples that whatever goes on between them behind closed doors is perfectly all right as long as it is mutually agreeable.

At one of my seminars I began to talk about oral sex, and out of the corner of my eye I saw a woman hit her husband in the ribs, as if to say, "I've heard enough, Harvey. Let's go home."

But old Harvey said something to her which, I'm pretty sure, was, "Wait a minute, Marge. I want to hear what he has to say."

Now I'm not suggesting that each of us goes out and incorporates oral sex into our marital relationship. I'm just using it as a way of challenging you to think about the fact that most of us bring mythical limits to the marriage partnership in general and the marriage bed in particular. But I have seen couples transcend these mythical limits and reach a more satisfying marriage. There is nothing wrong or dirty in two people sharing each other sexually, as long as it is a loving, giving act. The man's mission in marriage is to meet the needs of his wife, and the wife's mission is to meet the needs of her husband, in sex as in every other aspect of life.

I know that many of us were brought up in homes where it was conveyed that sex is bad, that our genitals are dirty, that we're never supposed to touch each other or our own selves. I have counseled many women especially, who are still trying to cope with what their well-meaning parents did to them when they were kids, which was to give them tremendous hang-ups about sex.

There is no sense in telling children in any way, shape, or form that sex is bad. Sex is beautiful, sex is good, sex is a God-given capability that each of us can enjoy. However, like any other privilege we have in life, it has guidelines that go along with it. We can't just go around acting on our feelings all the time. Sex is all that it can and should be only when it is surrounded by and wrapped in love.

Think back, for example, to the most pleasurable sexual experience you've ever had. That special time with your husband or wife that was absolutely *the* greatest. Chances are that it came at a time when the foundation was laid for sexual love to take place—an occasion when the husband and wife had been caring and attentive toward each other the entire day. But at the same time, it is also likely that the physical and emotional time together just happened. It was a spontaneous, loving moment—which grew out of that day full of caring actions.

For those who have had feelings of guilt associated with sex, it will take some time to be able to work their way back to where they can and ought to be in their marital relationship. But it can be done, and it's very much worth the effort. If both partners in a marriage don't work at becoming one, then the marriage may be threatened by still another game, and that is:

## TAKE THAT, YOU RAT!

Another name for this game might be, "If I can't get what I want from you, then I'll get it somewhere else!"

Of course, I'm talking about extramarital affairs. Depending on which survey you read, upward of 50 percent of married Americans have been unfaithful to their spouses—and I think that's a horrible statistic.

I've heard some people say that an affair can be good for a marriage, but I've never seen a shred of evidence that it's true. Anyone who walks eyes-open into an affair would be better advised to do something a bit safer, such as wrestling alligators in the swamps of Florida. Anyone who thinks, "No one will get hurt, and no one has to find out about it," doesn't know reality. No matter how it starts, an affair is more than likely going to turn into a raging forest fire of a thing that destroys everything in its path. And even if no one finds out, it leaves its participants with broken hearts, divided loyalties, and a load of guilt that's even too heavy for Arnold Schwarzenegger to bench press.

My advice is to avoid even the slightest opportunity for an affair to begin.

I remember the time that a prominent businessman called and made an appointment for himself and his wife. He told me over the phone that they had a few "minor" communication problems. He didn't think it was anything serious, really, but that maybe some professional assistance would help them sort things out. He insisted, however, that he meet with me first. I told him that wasn't the way I liked to work, but that in this instance I would defer to his better judgment.

Ed was a successful businessman, but even more than that, he was wrapped up in his work as an elder in his church. As he sat and told me about all his involvements on behalf of the church, I found it hard to believe that he had any time left to devote to his business, much less his marriage. And yet when he spoke of his wife, Kathy, his eyes glowed with pride. It was obvious that he loved her very much.

He said that she was beautiful, warmhearted, capable, a good mother and wife, although somewhat "immature."

When I pressed him for what he meant by this, he explained that she was not very understanding of his many commitments—particularly within the church and business community.

He also explained that there had been a number of petty issues lately that had mushroomed into some full-grown squabbles, and he felt there needed to be some "minor adjustments" within their relationship.

By now it was evident that this couple had a competitive marriage, and when I met Kathy at our second session, I saw quickly just how competitive it was. They both had a great deal of interest in proving who was right and who was wrong in every situation. And when somebody wins, somebody else has to lose.

I felt the need to have the next appointment with Kathy alone. And, in classical fashion, five minutes before the end of our session, she dropped the bomb. She said, "Well, I suppose if this is going to do any good, I'd better tell you the truth."

The "truth" was that Kathy was having an affair with someone in the church, right under her "elder" husband's nose, and he didn't have the slightest indication. (Take That, You Rat!) He was so busy and so totally absorbed in the church that he had neglected to take seriously his responsibilities to his wife. If he had done a better job of being attentive to her needs, she never would have become involved in an affair.

It was interesting that when Kathy talked to me about the gentleman with whom she was having the affair, she described him in terms that would indicate that he was easy to talk to and that he was a listener. He took the time to hear her and seemed to value what she said. Comparing that with Ed's style, it wasn't difficult to see why he was so attractive to her.

As we began to go back into Kathy's life at our next session, she gradually developed a greater trust and ability to be open with me. She admitted that she had had two prior affairs, all within the church and all right under her husband's nose. She felt guilty about them, but at this point I felt that the most important thing I could do was to show her that there were some logical reasons why she had sought out these illicit relationships. Again, I'm not saying that an affair is ever right, just that when someone is having one, there is bound to be a reason for it. Whatever needs are being met in the affair are usually the same needs that are being neglected within the marriage.

Kathy felt that she counted only when she was being noticed, when everyone was paying attention to her. This was an almost neurotic need in her life. And in what job was her husband doing the absolute worst? That of paying some attention to his beautiful and talented wife.

Kathy was tormented about whether to tell her husband what she had done, but in this case I thought that it would only create undue stress on their relationship. It might be something that he would not be able to handle. One thing I told her that she had to do, though, was make a new commitment to Ed.

Ed and Kathy finally got their marriage together with the help of a beautiful forty-four-hour weekend Marriage Encounter. And Kathy decided that she would bury her affairs once and for all. In order to do this, she had to approach the three men with whom she had had affairs. She asked for forgiveness from each of them for her part in initiating the affair, and then also expressed forgiveness to them. This helped to alleviate much of the guilt she had within her. Before the conclusion of their great weekend together, she and Ed made a new commitment to each other, to always put each other's needs first. They concluded the weekend by repeating their marriage vows while in each other's arms.

Marriage Encounter is offered through the Lutheran, Methodist, Catholic, Jewish, and other faiths, and I recommend it to interested couples who have a good marriage. It is not recommended as therapy for deeply troubled marriages; marriage counseling is still the best route to go for these. But if you are interested in Marriage Encounter, a few phone calls to area churches should provide you with information about the next such weekend in your area.

## Dump Truck

Another dangerous and dirty game that couples play with each other is called Dump Truck, and it's just like the name sounds. It works this way:

"I've got my dump truck full of all kinds of stinky, rotten garbage, and if you dump on me, you'd better know that it's coming right back at you."

It's a game of tit for tat, which can rapidly escalate into an all-out war. Sadly enough, the couples who play this game soon find themselves completely buried under all the garbage.

Many times I see couples who have gone through this dumping process over a long period of time, and then, when they reach down and try to feel something toward each other, they come up empty. My comment is usually along the lines of, "Yeah, I can see why you wouldn't feel anything. Does it have anything to do with the fact that you've got sixteen cubic yards of garbage covering your relationship?"

If you or your spouse has been in the habit of dumping on each other, now is the time to make a commitment to change your habits, before your marriage sinks to the depths to which Katie and Ron's marriage had sunk.

I could always tell when this couple was coming to the office, because I'd hear the four-letter words echoing down the hallway. That's how they related to each other, and I'm not exaggerating when I tell you that they were in the worst shape of any couple I had ever counseled. In their three and a half years of marriage Katie had twelve affairs that she could at least attach a name to and numerous one-night stands whose names somehow escaped her. Having affairs was her way of dumping on her husband.

But don't go thinking that she was any blond bombshell. Far from it. She packed at least 245 pounds on that five-foot-four-inch frame of hers, but she was still able to find plenty of willing partners. Because Ron was six three and probably didn't weigh much more than 150 pounds, they always presented a comical sight as they walked across the parking lot toward my office—like some profane Mutt and Jeff, swearing up a storm at each other.

But their problems weren't comical at all.

In addition to her sexual escapades, Katie was a power-ful woman with an explosive temper. On more than one occasion she had punched her fist through the plasterboard walls of their home. While she tended to be explosive, her husband was passive. These two were opposites in just about every sense of the word.

Occasionally in therapy, clients will get the idea that the therapist is pitting one mate against the other, and one evening Katie thought that I was doing just that. She became very angry, called me a nasty name, and proceeded to leave the office in a huff, slamming the door behind her. (At least she didn't take a swing at me or punch her fist through one of *my* walls.) She was determined that she was going to walk home, even though she lived eight miles from the office, just to show us that she was the boss. She wanted us to know that we had made her feel uncom-fortable and guilty and we were going to pay.

Ron immediately sprang to his feet to chase after her, but I literally grabbed him by the seat of his pants and told

205

him to sit down. Then I asked him, "Is this typical? Is this the kind of thing that goes on in your home?"

Yes, he said, it was. She was always throwing tantrums of one sort or another.

I told him that if things were going to turn around in his marriage, he'd better begin behaving differently, and that there was no time to start like the present.

He was nervous about it, I could tell, but he agreed that he would let her walk home.

Katie left the office like a steamroller with a full head of steam. She took off, waddling down the street, eyes staring straight ahead. In the back of her mind she probably *knew* Ron wouldn't be too far behind, telling her how sorry he was and begging her to get in the car with him. Only that's not what happened. She walked and walked, and walked some more, and there was still no sign of her husband.

At an intersection about a mile from my office, something happened to Katie. She walked into the abyss. Actually, she fell into a construction hole and broke her leg in two places. She lay there until sometime after two in the morning, when someone finally heard her cry for help. Assistance was called, and Katie was transported to the nearest hospital for emergency treatment.

Meanwhile, Ron was at home, asleep in bed. He had no idea where his wife was, but that wasn't such an unusual situation, and he had given no thought to the possibility that she might be in danger. In the hours just before dawn he was awakened by the telephone, and a voice on the other end asked him if he could come to the hospital right away, because his wife had broken her leg.

Ron said, "I'll be right there," hung up, and began hurriedly dressing. But then he started thinking, "What would Leman suggest?" And he finally decided to go back to bed and get a few more hours of sleep.

It wasn't until 10 A.M. that Ron finally sauntered into Katie's hospital room. Unfortunately, her mood hadn't been greatly improved by lying in a hole for several hours with a broken leg. Her first words to her husband were, "When I get out of here, I'm going to break your little neck!"

But she didn't. And to this day, Katie says it was this particular incident that triggered the much-needed changes in the couple's relationship.

Now you might be thinking that Katie was totally to blame for the problems in her marriage. But that was not the case. Dump Truck is a two-person game, and they were both taking part. For example, Ron's favorite dumping was using a large vocabulary, which he knew Katie wouldn't understand. He had a degree from a community college, while she had only an eighth-grade education. He seemed to enjoy those instances when Katie appeared to be confused and ignorant. She handled those "put-downs" by giving herself to so many men she couldn't possibly remember all their names. Her private logic was, "If you have the right to put me down, then I have the right to get back at you." But revenge is a two-edged sword. You may hurt someone else when you use it, but you're likely to hurt yourself too.

If you and your mate have been playing Dump Truck for a while, then it's time for one of you, if not both of you, to care enough to take some action toward change.

The most dangerous signal that your marriage is in trouble is when you simply don't care one way or another about what is taking place in your relationship.

Ron and Katie's marriage shows how important it is to make a commitment to change. But remember that you can never change your partner. You cannot stop the alcoholic from taking a drink, the overindulgent eater from wolfing down an extra burger and fries. In fact you cannot make another adult do anything he doesn't want to do. That's why the change and commitment must start within you. Ron and Katie were miles apart emotionally when they made the decision to seek therapy together. Ron's commitment to remove his sails from Katie's wind by doing the unexpected was the action that precipitated change.

Where does a marriage counselor begin to deal with a marriage as "hopeless" as theirs was? First, I asked them if they ever stopped dumping on each other. Ron's response was, "Yeah! During and after sex!"

"Fine, then we're going to start there."

"Where?" he asked.

I said, "Right there. In your home, when you're having sex. The next time I want you to just hold each other and thank the Lord for your crummy relationship!" (Well . . . we had to start someplace.)

Realizing that even beautiful cathedrals are built one brick at a time, Ron and Katie slowly began to build a better relationship. These days I have a very special photo of Ron and Katie in my office. That's because after several months of intensive therapy, they came to my office and gave me a picture of the two of them, big smiles on their faces, arms wrapped around each other. They handed me the photo and Katie said, "Dr. Leman, this is for your office. I want you to think of us when other couples come for help. Feel free to tell them our story."

I have. And I will continue to do so. If there was ever a marriage that seemed to be beyond hope, it was theirs. And yet they made it. There's no such thing as hopeless.

The day they brought the photo by for me, their new-found "coupleness" was a beautiful thing to see. They had just come from Wal-Mart, where they had bought a new set of dishes—which they needed because they had broken most of their other dishes by throwing them at each other. Katie had also been faithfully taking part in

Weight Watchers for eight months and had lost a whopping one hundred pounds. Her ideas about herself and about life in general were changing, and those changes were manifesting themselves in every aspect of her being—emotionally, physically, and spiritually.

Her attitude was much, much better, and it showed.

It was just too bad that Ron and Katie had to learn so many things the hard way, but then I suppose that is true of most of us—which reminds me of the story of the lion, the donkey, and the fox that went on a rampage through the jungle, killing everything in sight. After a two-and-a-half-hour killing spree the lion decided it was time to rest, so he asked the donkey to divide the prey equally among the three of them. After the donkey completed his work, the lion became enraged, clawed the donkey to death, and ate him.

He then turned to the fox and said, "Mr. Fox, would you please divide the prey fairly?" The sly old fox went over and took a mangy bird and put it in front of himself while he moved all the rest of the game in front of the lion. The pleased lion looked at the fox and said, "Mr. Fox! Where did you learn to divide so fairly and so evenly?"

The fox looked up and said, "The donkey taught me."

It's true, isn't it, that many of us—as husbands, wives, and lovers—learn the hard way.

## CHILDREN ARE THE ENEMY

The first time I heard a psychologist say, "Children are the enemy," I thought to myself, "Oh boy, here's another wacko psychologist making another off-the-wall remark about children." At that time I didn't have any children. I have since learned—as much as I love my children and as convinced as I am that I wouldn't trade a single one of them for anything in the universe—that those words are true: Children *are* the enemy.

This game pits you not against your spouse, but against those darling little creatures that I like to think of as "ankle biters": your children.

It usually goes something like this:

There you are in your living room with your spouse. You finally got the kids to bed, and now it's time for some quiet talk between just the two of you. You love your children, but ah . . . isn't it peaceful once they're tucked into bed for the night?

Well, that's what *you* think. Because at this very moment the darlings are not in bed at all, but gathering at the top of the stairs, whispering and planning their attack.

Right now the general and the colonel—meaning the eleven-year-old and the nine-year-old—are giving their instructions to the corporal—the three-year-old: "Herbie . . . you go in there and tell Mom and Dad that you're hungry and want something to eat. Go on . . . get out there. Scoot." Little Herbie begins to shuffle his feet toward the living room, blankey in tow. He's so cute—he looks just like your father. But your first instinct when you see that little spittin' image out of his bed is—*kill him!*

But you don't kill him. In fact, if you're like most parents you probably say, "Okay, one quick snack and right into bed." But almost before the words are out of your mouth, two more shadows appear in the hallway, rubbing their eyes and acting as if Herbie woke them up. But as long as they *are* up now, of course, they're hungry too.

Score the first round to the children.

Another time you and your spouse may be sitting together on the couch, just enjoying the peace and quiet, when you suddenly hear thumping, bumping, and scraping, followed by a loud boom and a scream from your seven-year-old, who sleeps in the same room with his older brother.

The scream is your cue to jump up and run into their room, angrily asking the question no parent in history has ever gotten an honest answer to . . . namely, "What's going on in here?"

Naturally, both kids are pointing at each other and saying things like, "He started it!" "Did not! He did." After a few exchanges of this sort, you just say, "I don't know who started it and I don't really care. But you two go to sleep . . . right now!" Then you storm back out of the room—but, of course, the pleasant mood that you were feeling earlier is completely gone, and you can feel the pounding begin inside your head.

Second round goes to the children.

You see, children are the enemy because anything that comes between the husband and wife is the enemy. Now there are several areas in family life where children are likely to attack, and I want to talk specifically about four of them:

*1. They will control your life if you'll let them.*

If you're not careful, you'll soon find that everything you do, twenty-four hours a day, is regulated by your children. You'll be fixing your meals when they want to eat and serving the things they like to eat. You'll be watching the television programs they want to watch, and you'll be planning your free time around their schedules. You'll be letting them monopolize the conversation.

And that's not the way it should be. Yes, children are important, and yes their likes and dislikes, schedules, and feelings should all be taken into consideration. But the most important relationship in the family is the one between husband and wife, and that's the one that has to take priority.

That's one of the reasons I am constantly urging married couples to go away every once in a while for a romantic weekend together—to recharge their batteries and recommit themselves to each other. It's not only good for the couple but for the children as well, who see that their mom and dad always put their marriage above any other family consideration.

*2. They will monopolize your time.*

When Dad—or Mom—comes home from work at six, all the kids run to him with hugs and kisses, anxious to tell him about their day. The wise parent, after giving the love and kisses and greetings, will ask for some time out for just a few minutes to wind down. Then the time he spends with his children, even if it's only a few minutes before dinner, will at least be productive time. The other spouse needs to help protect that necessary winding-down time. Also, the mother who spends all day at home with her children must be sure to get away occasionally during the day. She should be able to hire a sitter and go out to lunch, a meeting, etc. If Mom also happens to be working all day, she usually doesn't get to punch out until 10 P.M., while Dad checks out of the family pretty soon after the evening meal. That's the old double standard at work, and it's not fair. (Have you ever heard Dad tell some of the "boys" that he had to "baby-sit" the kids? How come when Mom does it, hour after hour, she's just fulfilling her role as a mother, but when Dad does it for a single evening he's "baby-sitting"?) Mom and Dad both need some time for themselves as individuals, as well as time together as a couple.

*3. They will control your sex life.*

One question I am frequently asked at seminars is, "How do other couples find privacy for their sex life?"

Yes, it was easy to find time when the kids were little, but when they get older and have more time to themselves, there is an increasing possibility of their interrupting their parents' time together.

I remember one rather rotund woman who shared that she and her husband were enjoying themselves in the bedroom when they fell out of bed and made a terrible crash. The teenagers ran into the bedroom to see what had happened, and there, in all their naked glory, were Mom and Dad, sprawled on the floor. (Whoops! Should've locked the door!)

Many married people are extremely self-conscious about making love while their children are awake. They're afraid that their children will "hear something." So I tell them if that's what they're afraid of, turn up the stereo or the radio. And if a couple really feels uncomfortable about making love when the kids are in the house and awake, what's wrong with taking a motel room for an evening? That can be very romantic and add some pizzazz back into your marriage.

One time I was traveling with my wife on a business trip. Sande and I were enjoying being together, sitting close to one another, holding hands, etc., and I began to feel quite amorous. I suggested that we stop at a motel, even though it was the middle of the day. To my great pleasure, she said okay, so that's what we did.

We were on our way up the steps to the lobby when we began to howl with laughter because we realized that we didn't have any luggage. What would people think? Sande went back to the car and got her little plastic knitting bag to carry in with us. Somehow it made her feel better, but I wondered what anybody who might have been watching thought about us.

But it doesn't matter! We had a good time.

Some might think that spending money on a motel room is frivolous and that you should be able to control your passions until you can have some privacy at home. But I disagree, and I can't think of a better investment to make than in your relationship with your marital partner.

213

One of the reasons parents let their children interfere with their sexual relationship is that they pretend that they don't have sexual feelings, and that's not right. Your kids need to know that Mommy and Daddy love each other and like to hold and kiss each other.

I realize that talking about sex can be difficult. But the best way to handle it is to open up and share your feelings with your children. The truth is that your children will either learn about sex from you in a healthy, marriage-related manner or they will learn about it somewhere else, and they may come to see it in a filthy and degrading way.

*4. They will divide and conquer.*

Children are sensitive to any division there might be between their moms and dads, and they will do their best to exploit that division to their own advantage.

I urge you to develop "couple power," or your children will take advantage of any little differences that you and your spouse have. Have you ever noticed how many times children will aggravate a situation to get you and your mate at each other's throats? And it works. Why? Because you haven't come together as one in your marriage. Let your children see that you are united. If an issue comes up—and it will—where you have different feelings about how a matter should be handled, go behind closed doors and discuss it. Then come out, united, and give the children your decision.

One area where children often are able to divide and conquer is in the area of discipline. Jay Kesler in his book *Too Big to Spank* has this to say about discipline:

> To be united in our approach to rules and discipline provides a sense of confidence. Teens become unsure and apprehensive if they do not have guidelines. If they sense that we are agreed and unified they are spared the insecurity of too much freedom. . . . Our experience has been that when

we are not careful in the mutual understanding of rules we tend to have arguments. An agreement ahead of time is the best way to avoid misunderstanding later.[12]

If united discipline is not practiced in your household, a good time to launch such a program is during the dinner hour when you are all together. The attitude for this tactic is arbitration. Explain that you feel it is necessary that some house rules be established so that everyone will understand where he stands. Get some input from your kids as to what rules ought to be instituted in the family. This kind of meeting where everybody gets a chance to pitch in and have input is the democratic way. Problems can be hashed out and solved in a logical and straightforward manner; much better than if Mommy and Daddy talk it over and make all the decisions. In this way, you have a better chance of winning the enemy over to your side.

Some additional family matters that can be discussed in family meetings are: where you are going to spend your vacation together next summer, who does what chores, how to resolve conflicts between family members.

## WHO'S NUMBER ONE?

I'm sure I could describe several more destructive games that couples play in a competitive marriage. Perhaps you and your spouse are playing a game right now—one that I mentioned or one you have thought up all by yourselves. All "games" are threatening to your marriage, because if there is a winner then there has to be a loser. And the winner becomes the loser too, because he or she is likely to lose the entire marriage.

The most important thing is that you keep your marriage in general and your spouse in particular at the top of your list of priorities.

In his book *Traits of a Happy Couple,* Larry Halter gives several steps couples can take to strengthen their marriages, and I want to briefly consider two positive "games" couples can play. These are "Care Day" and "Cookie Jar" and they work like this:[13]

### CARE DAY

The idea here is to set up a day in which it is your job to increase the number of positive things you do for your mate. If you're a typical husband, you probably remember your wife's birthday, your wedding anniversary, Mother's Day, and Valentine's Day, and that's about it. If you ever sent her flowers for no reason except that you love her, she'd probably think you were up to something. But just think of how pleased she'd be, once she understood that you did it just to say, "I love you."

If you're a typical wife, you've probably never thought much about doing something like having "I love you" balloons sent to your husband's office just to let him know you're thinking about him. But wouldn't it make him feel good if you did?

A Care Day is a day when you choose to shower your spouse with good things. For example, if you are able to do so, you might take an hour or two off from work in the morning so you and your spouse can go out and have breakfast together. Perhaps you'll want to send flowers during the day and plan dinner at a nice restaurant for that evening. Or maybe it's nothing that elegant. Maybe it's taking her to her mother's house for a visit that evening and being as pleasant as can be about it—even if you'd really rather get into the ring against Mike Tyson. Perhaps it's taking an evening to tackle all of those chores around the house that she's been nagging you about for so long.

Whatever your Care Day consists of, it must be things that will bring pleasure to your spouse and show him or her how much you care.

And if an entire Care Day seems to be too much for you, start off smaller with a Care Evening or even a Care Hour. Just keep in mind that the goal is to please your spouse.

### COOKIE JAR

This game, which is also designed to increase the number of positive exchanges between husbands and wives, consists of preparing lists of things you'd like your spouse to do for you. The idea is to write things on different colored slips of paper—for instance, yellow for the wife and green for the husband—one item per one piece of paper, and to put them in a cookie jar or similar container.

Then, every day, each of you should take one of your spouse's items out of the jar and resolve to do that thing for him or her. Dr. Halter gives these guidelines for using the cookie jar:

> First, the desired events should not include requests for sweeping personality changes like "Be an extrovert." Second, the requests should ask for an increase in a behavior, not a decrease. Events like "Stop smoking" or "Don't yell at the kids" won't work. Third, you need to put the Cookie Jar in an easy-to-see place so it'll be a constant reminder to use it.[14]

Remember that the things you write down for your spouse to do for you must be reasonable. You might include things such as:

Take me for a walk in the park.
Take me out to a romantic movie.
Take me out for dinner.

Give me a back rub.
Help me wash the car.
Make love to me.
Go away with me for the weekend.
Take a shower with me.

I'm sure you get the idea, which is to create a positive exchange between you and your loved one. It's important to open up to your mate and say, "Here are some things that would make me happy," and playing the game of Cookie Jar is one way to do it without feeling that you're being demanding or asking for too much. At the same time, it lets you know some definite things you can do that will bring pleasure to your spouse—just in case your own creative juices are running a bit low.

In the first chapter of this book I admonished you to make your spouse number one on your list of priorities, and I have been constantly reinforcing that idea. I guarantee you that if you put each other first in your marriage—if you know what your needs are and what your mate's needs are, and you both make a 100 percent effort to meet those needs—then you're going to have a happy marriage. It will be a marriage that is fulfilling and rewarding for you in every respect. Your marriage is going to be the winner and no one will ever read your name in the divorce column of the daily newspaper!

Every year or so, I do something special for Sande, taking her out to dinner and then to a hotel. She was so funny the first time I did this—she had no clue as to what to expect.

After dinner I drove to the hotel, but she refused to get out of the car. "I don't have any luggage," she protested. "How will it look?"

I finally coaxed her out of the car and into a side entrance. You see, I had already been there earlier that day, renting the room and preparing it. There were five pink roses beside the king-size bed, one for each of our children, and two books on the nightstand. Sande was totally paranoid at this point. What was I planning?

From under the bed, I pulled a little suitcase of her things I had packed earlier. Then I told her to relax. I tucked her in, kissed her goodnight, and said I'd order room service on the way out (the gooiest, chocolatiest dessert on the menu). I promised to pick her up the next morning for breakfast.

I must say, this required a great deal of restraint on my part. Here's the woman I love, in bed, no kids around to bother us. But I knew that Sande would appreciate the time alone, she needed that time, and it was the most loving gift I could give her.

As I said, I've done this every year or so since then. Sure, we have our times *together,* but this gift of time alone is something Sande cherishes, and she loves me for giving it to her.

## Action, Not Words

Take a piece of paper and rank your ten most important priorities in life, and get your spouse to do the same thing.

Once you've finished, compare lists. What do they tell you about your relationship with each other? What things do you have to change? If your job is the most important thing in your life, you are not going to be happy in your marriage. Big businesses are beginning to realize that the employee who puts his job before his home life is not as effective as the one who has a happy, fulfilling marriage. Now I know that some of you are thinking, "Yeah, but you don't understand. My job is really important. In my line of work my job has to be my top priority."

Baloney. Not to get you prematurely to your final resting place, but what would happen at your job if you died today? How long do you think it would be before your replacement could be where you left off? After they passed the hat in the office or made a donation to your favorite charity, life would go on. Anyone who thinks that he's indispensable is going to receive a rude awakening sooner or later.

If your children are in the number-one position in your life, what is going to happen to your marriage when you find yourself in an empty nest?

You cannot put your husband or wife in the #2 (or lower) position. Your marital partner must always be the top priority in your life, your children should be number two, and your job number three, at best.

If you and your spouse are playing some games that are destructive to your marriage, you might want to try the game of Marital Baseball. All you need is three columns on a piece of paper. At the top of the first column write "innings." Underneath, number down from one to seven (there will be seven innings in this "baseball" game—one for each day of the week). At the top of the other two columns put an H (for husband) and W (for wife)—or use your initials if you want to, it really doesn't matter. Tape your baseball scorecard to the refrigerator door, and every time one of you dumps on the other or does something to reinforce the concept of "I win, you lose," give yourself a score—one, two, or three runs each inning. If you haven't scored all day, give yourself a big goose egg and congratulate yourself. The idea here is to have increasing numbers of zeros on your scorecard because, unlike real baseball, it's the lowest score that wins in this game, and your objective is to have both of you win!

# 11

## Ying-Yangs, Weenies, Tallywackers, and "The Thing"

People were still filing into the huge auditorium as I began to speak on the topic "What Every Parent Ought to Know about Sex." After a very nice introduction and a warm reception, I turned to the audience and said, "What do we call penises in our society?"

Silence . . . dead silence! One lady in the front row elbowed her husband and seemed to ask, "Harry, is he talking about piano players or what?"

I'm sure she was hoping that I had said "pianists" instead of "penises," but I hadn't.

I decided that I'd try again. "Come on, what do we call penises in our society? Better yet, what did your mother call your penis, men?" Finally, after not getting any response, I asked for a show of hands. Any suggestions?

Slowly hands began to go up all over the auditorium. "Peter," somebody said. "Weenie," somebody else volunteered.

Now they were warming up to the task.

"Pecker!" "Pokey!" "The thing!"

Now the names were coming in fast succession: "Ying-yang (is that a Chinese pecker?), dork, dink, pee-wee, John-ston . . ." By this time the crowd was nearly hysterical with laughter. Some of them were laughing so hard they were crying. They were also immensely enjoying telling me their life secrets. Some of these fellows had ditty-whackers, tallywackers, ding-dongs, and others had schwantzes, tee-tees, and thing-a-majigs. At this point, I didn't even know if I was going to be able to get to the rest of the evening.

But what do these cute and funny nicknames tell us about our feelings toward sex? I believe this is a way we manifest our discomfort when we talk about sexual subjects. We dress them up with cute nicknames or euphemisms because the "real" words are too dirty or suggestive.

Most of us have a difficult time talking explicitly about sexual matters to each other as husbands and wives and to our children. Letha Scanzoni, in her book *Sex Is a Parent Affair,* says that there is no reason

> that a male toddler, who points to various parts of his body and hears his parents say, "nose," "eye," "hand," "toe," should suddenly hear strange euphemisms when he points to his genital area and hears "pee-pee," "pee-wee," "wee-nie," "teapot," "periwinkle," to cite only a few. Then he soon learns that he is never to use the word around any-one outside the home. The correct name, of course, is *penis,* and the saclike structure under it is the *scrotum* and contains his *testicles.*[15]

I made an appearance once on *Good Morning America* to discuss "Teaching Kids about Sex." I have to tell you, whenever I appear on a nationwide broadcast like that, I always feel pressured to hit a home run. And my personal gauge of success is the crew. If I can get those camera operators and lighting technicians to laugh uncontrollably, I've done okay.

Anyway, this time I told the story of something that happened when my youngest daughter, Lauren, was only three. I was in the bathroom, uh, "going potty," you might say, when somehow Lauren walked in and surprised me. She pointed and said, "What's that?" I hoped she was talking about my watch.

"Oh, that's just Daddy's watch," I replied.

"No," she said, pointing again. "That!"

I gulped and said, "That's Daddy's penis."

On *Good Morning America* I explained that I could have called it a ying-yang, weenie, tallywacker, little big man, little joe, or in Spanish, *pistola de agua*. As I went on with these names the crew was in stitches, and I knew I had done well. I understand they were still talking about that spot weeks later.

But the point remains: Those cute names just demonstrate our discomfort. They're funny to listen to, and they can sure crack up an audience, but when you're teaching your kids, use the right words.

## LACK OF PROPER SEX EDUCATION

Most of us were taught early in childhood that sex is bad, dirty, and a subject never to be discussed in "nice company." Think about your own childhood. How did you learn about sex? Did you learn about it from a warm, open, and loving discussion with your mom and dad, with them sitting down together and sharing part of their love life with you? I seriously doubt it. It's more likely that at some point

223

in your life your mom said to your dad, "You're going to have to have a talk with your son—or daughter—about the birds and the bees." At which point your dad told you, "Er . . . ah . . . your mother wants to talk to you."

If you are a woman, during your preteen years Mom or your gym teacher at school or your family doctor probably took just long enough to tell you about the advent of the monthly menstrual cycle. Of course, your more mature girlfriends had already shared this news with you, but someone had to let you know what to do hygienically when this exciting, yet frightening, situation occurred.

But the actual nitty-gritty about the sexual relationship between male and female came to most of us from "knowledgeable" friends, dirty stories, and things written on the walls of public restrooms.

According to the couples I see in private practice, only about 2 percent of them had what they considered to be adequate sex education. These fortunate people had an early exposure to matters of sex, centered around Mom and Dad passing information, feelings, ideas, and values to their children. One of the reasons your parents never talked to you about sex is that no one ever talked with them about it either. Being kept in the dark was the acceptable way of life.

Let's get back to the auditorium again. People were still laughing when I asked the next question: "Now what did you call the female genitalia?" For the second time that evening, a deep hush came over the audience, which had been on the edge of hysteria moments before. I began to push, "Okay, come on! What do we call the female genitalia?"

Finally one woman volunteered, "We didn't call it anything in our home; we just didn't refer to it at all. It was like it wasn't there." A well-built, stocky man who looked like a Marine Corps sergeant spoke up in a loud voice,

"Well, I'd tell you, Doc, but I don't think I should tell you here."

One of the reasons why this man felt that way is that most of the names we have for the female genitalia are "down there." They're dirty, nasty, derogatory names. Now why is it that the names for the male genitalia are funny, but the female references are not at all amusing?

## SUPERIOR-INFERIOR ATTITUDE

Imagine that we're in the locker room at a high school, listening as the guys come in from their basketball practice. One guy yells across the locker room, "Hey, Charlie! What'd you 'get' last night?" Charlie will respond that he "got" this, or a little bit of that or that he almost scored.

Just think for a moment about the words these guys are using for sex. Terms like *score* and *get* or *conquest*. Do these sound like loving, caring terms, or do they seem far removed from the special feelings we should have toward someone with whom we are involved in a love relationship? These young people are learning that sexual relationships are competitive. Their idea about sex is that it's a taking-from rather than a giving-to experience. The question seems to be, "How much can I get for myself?" and not "How much can I give to the other person?" This is one of the results of the early teaching that sex is bad, dirty, and an undiscussable subject. Naturally, forbidden fruit is all the more desirable; hence the competitive attitude.

These young people are approaching sex as if it's a competition, a place where somebody has to win and somebody has to lose.

I'm not telling any secrets when I say that men in our society have traditionally had a superior attitude about their sexual relationship with women. To illustrate this truth, think of a dirty story for just a second. Who gets the brunt of the joke? I've asked this question hundreds of times in seminars across the country, and I've learned that in a huge majority of cases it's the woman who is the subject of the humor. This is further evidence that our male-oriented society has come in many instances to the place of viewing women as "sex objects," as "things" to be used. But women are not for using. Women are for loving. You see, any time sex is used as a weapon to conquer or overcome feelings of inferiority, to repay a favor, to perform a duty, to gain attention or power, or to win a battle in marriage, it is not going to be fulfilling to the couple. As a matter of fact, it probably won't be fulfilling for either partner. In the best sexual relationships there are no superior/inferior roles—but mutual love and respect.

Some people may say that it's old-fashioned to insist that fulfilling sex can stem only from a deep love for your partner, but my answer to that is that in some instances the old ways were better. Much better. In fact, when it comes to the subject of love, I've yet to find anything that speaks with the eloquence or truthfulness of a very old source. That source is the Bible, and specifically 1 Corinthians 13:4–8, 13:

> Love is patient, love is kind. It does not envy, it does not boast, it is not proud. It is not rude, it is not self-seeking, it is not easily angered, it keeps no record of wrongs. Love does not delight in evil but rejoices with the truth. It always protects, always trusts, always hopes, always perseveres.
>
> Love never fails. But where there are prophecies, they will cease; where there are tongues, they will be stilled, where there is knowledge, it will pass away. . . .
>
> And now these three remain: faith, hope and love. But the greatest of these is love.

Husbands and wives who learn the reality of these words, and who live by them, will have joyous, fulfilling marriages.

I want to try to drive home two very important truths about romantic relationships between men and women. They are:

1. Men and women are different.
2. Sex really *does* begin in the kitchen.

Now, as to the first point, you may be saying, "Tell us something we don't already know."

But then, I'm not just talking about the obvious—the differences in superstructure. There are profound differences in every aspect of the makeup of men and women, and the sad truth is that most men don't understand women at all.

For example, if I asked a thousand men, "What is the most special physical act a man can engage in with a woman?" I'd probably get a response of leering laughter, catcalls, and statements such as, "Boy, if you don't know that, I feel sorry for you!"

The problem is that if I ask women that same question I am going to get a completely different answer. Men think that sexual intercourse is the most special physical act, while a woman will say the most special act is just being held and holding on to the man she loves. We get into difficulty in marriage when we begin thinking that sexual intercourse is the most important thing. A husband who doesn't understand that his wife needs him to express his love for her by holding her close to him, gently and tenderly, is not going to have a happy and fulfilled wife, no matter how much of an "artist" he may fancy himself to be when it comes to sex.

Am I saying that women don't enjoy sex? Not at all. A woman who has a partner who makes her feel loved and cherished is capable of receiving immense pleasure from sexual love. But still, there is something in her soul that longs more for the intimacy of being held than for the thrill of sexual contact.

Another way men and women are different is that men are much more readily aroused by sight than are women. That is why magazines depicting nude women continue to flourish. However, magazines published for women depicting nude men will never have the staying power and interest that "men's magazines" have. Women are less likely to be sexually aroused by a good-looking man walking by or by a nude man.

In fact, at one point the most successful such magazine for women, *Playgirl*, announced that it was no longer going to print completely nude photographs of the men it features. The publishers explained that this wasn't really what their audience wanted anyway, and they must have been right, since their decision didn't cause any great outcry. But just imagine what would happen if *Playboy* suddenly announced that it was no longer going to print nude photos of beautiful women, since it had been determined that most men really did buy the magazine to read the articles. Well, you know as well as I do that there would be riots all over the place if Hugh Hefner made a decision like that.

A man's time clock may start ticking at the sight of an attractive female, a suggestive picture, or a seductive look. He is easily aroused by external stimuli, whereas most women aren't. My wife has always claimed that I am much sexier with my clothes on than off. I've never tried it, but some night I'm going to sneak under the covers in my best three-piece pinstripe suit and bellow my mating call.

Now don't think that I'm saying that some women are not aroused by the physical presence of men; that would be a ridiculous statement to make. But remember that the most meaningful act a husband can engage in with his wife is just to hold her. And any time he's willing to do that, without expecting it to lead to anything else, his wife is going to be in seventh heaven. I hope you're listening to me, guys!

Now I know that often, after I give a lecture on this topic, there are many men who go home and say, "You know, maybe Leman has something here. After all, Marge has been just a little bit cold for the last eighteen years, so I'm going to try it. I'm just going to hold her for a while."

So he takes Marge in his arms, and for a few seconds Marge is blissfully thinking, "This is wonderful! He finally woke up! He sees that this is what makes me feel special."

However, about 4.3 seconds later his little Black and Decker begins to crank up. All of a sudden those caveman impulses begin to take over: *"Woman! Woman! Me Tarzan, you Jane!"* and all of that.

What happens at this point is that her tender feelings toward her husband take a nosedive. She thinks, "Oh . . . so *that's* what he was really after. I should have known!" And her interest in sex and in just being close to her husband plummets to an all-time low.

Actually, though, that *wasn't* what he was after. It was just that once his engine started revving, it was difficult to cool his jets.

To begin to become one in marriage, to begin to meet each other's needs, we have to realize that men and women are different. Whereas the old man might begin to feel frisky after just 4.3 seconds, it might be 43 minutes before Marge is even vaguely in the mood to be loved. To offset these problems in marriage, the couple has to learn the skill of being close without having sexual intercourse. There need to be times when they can just cuddle up together, hold each other's hands, scratch each other's backs, rub each other's feet—just to be close, loving, and caring—but without bringing sex into it. Men like to be held too—and can learn, with practice, that it doesn't always have to lead to "the horizontal boogie."

At the same time, the woman in this situation needs to be patient and understanding of her husband's libidinous impulses and at least give him an E for effort if he's trying to move in the right direction.

Another way men and women are different in the area of sex is that women tend to need verbal rather than visual stimulation. This is because females, in general, are more verbally oriented than are men. They are generally better at expressing their feelings. They enjoy conversation more, and they are just flat-out more expressive.

If you think I'm off-base on this one, then check it out the next time you're at a social gathering in which men and women gravitate to different parts of the house. At a Christmas party, for example, the women may gather in the kitchen, while the men will sit in the den. First of all, listen to the sounds of talking and laughter coming out of the kitchen. And then listen to the sounds of conversation coming from the direction of the den. The difference will probably be like that between a machine gun and a six-shooter. Women are just better at talking.

And they can get fairly deep with each other pretty quickly. They'll be sharing their deepest emotions and experiences, while the men in the other room are still playing, "So . . . Charlie . . . what do you do for a living?" (Incidentally, this is one of the first questions a man asks when he meets another man. Part of it is due to the fact that we're sizing the other fellow up, and part of it may be due to the fact that we can't think of anything else to say. Anyway, you have to admit that "What do you do for a living?" is better than, "So, what do you think of this weather we're having?" or even that old standard, "Is it hot enough for you?")

Another indication of the fact that women need verbal stimulation is the vast number of romance novels being cranked out by book publishers worldwide. Writers like

Danielle Steel sell millions of such books every year, and it's not men who are buying them. Why are those books so popular? Is it the great plots of the stories? Yeah, right! And guys read *Playboy* for the interesting articles. No, it's because they contain beautiful images of romantic love—including numerous passages that are extremely explicit when it comes to the sex act itself.

The male hero of these books always burns with passion for the heroine. He would go anywhere, do anything, suffer any injustice in his effort to win her hand. And he expresses his love so eloquently—no wonder the leading female character finally falls into bed with him with such ease. And no wonder so many millions of female readers are sighing dreamily and wishing the men in their lives were more like the fantasy characters in the books they read.

What's my point? Simply that a woman needs to hear her man tell her how much he loves her. She needs him to tell her how thankful he is that she's a part of his life. She needs to know that she looks "exceptionally beautiful tonight," or that "I love you more today than I did on the day we were married." Do you think that your wife is "the most beautiful girl in the world"? Then tell her. Is being in bed with her the greatest feeling you've ever experienced? Then tell her that too, but keep in mind that you don't have to "talk sexy" to get her motor running.

Yes, it's true that women are better at expressing themselves, but that doesn't mean that we men can't learn to do better—especially with regard to telling the women in our lives how much we love them.

The second thing I want to talk about is the fact that sex really does begin in the kitchen. As I said in the first chapter, the traditional couple in America today has sex in the bedroom, sandwiched between the late news and the *David Letterman* show, with the lights out and the man on top of the woman. But sex doesn't have to be and shouldn't be relegated to the bedroom. It can and should happen in any room in the house. Sex can be in the living room, in front of the fireplace, outdoors, or even in the garage (but be careful of spiders). Sex can even be in the kitchen.

As a matter of fact, as I stated in the beginning of this book, fulfilling, gratifying sex often does begin in the kitchen. For a woman to come into full expression of her feelings there has to be a certain aura around the sexual union. That aura might start in the morning when the husband remembers to take the garbage out. Or when he remembers to pick up his dirty socks and underwear and put them into the hamper where they belong. Or with any other kind of small courtesy or kindness to his family. Sex is an all-day affair. It starts early in the morning and culminates at a later time in a healthy and loving way, providing the groundwork has been laid for the sexual union.

Many men have been in the business world too long. They keep talking about results. But sex isn't a business, and it can't be approached as if it were. Neither is sex a spectator sport where one party sits back and waits for the action to begin.

For sex to be mutually fulfilling it has to be exciting. When you've created the proper aura and conditions are just right, how do you proceed to make the sex act exciting? Is it in technique? This is what some husbands try to tell me. But the key element in making sex exciting is for a man to understand that he must be gentle, loving, and caring in all things. It's a matter of loving your wife, meeting her needs, and putting her priorities first in your life. It's a matter of being genuinely concerned about her, and letting her see that concern.

Marriage is sometimes like the man who pulled into a service station and told the attendant he had a flat tire. The attendant responded, "How's your generator?"

"My generator is fine. I have a flat tire. Would you fix my flat tire, please?"

"How's your carburetor?"

"My carburetor's fine. I have a flat tire. Now would you fix the flat? I have to be at the office in fifteen minutes."

My point is this: If we don't service the more *immediate* needs of our husband or wife, then we aren't going to have the opportunity to service the more intimate needs in his or her life. And don't ever dismiss the immediate needs as unimportant.

You have to build a track record, so to speak, to show your mate that you really do care about him or her. Many husbands make the mistake of thinking that the "little things" aren't important. But when a woman is home with small children all day, and the washing machine won't work, and the baby eats a dead bug off the rug, and the two-year-old gets into the oil paint, don't ever dismiss the "little things" as not being important! If your wife spent three hours trying to get that green paint off her favorite white bedspread, she needs to know that you care. She wants to know that you are interested in the trials and triumphs of her everyday life.

## The Act of Love

Most of the men I see are lousy lovers.

Why? Because not only do they fail to understand that sex begins in the kitchen, but they really don't know much about the actual sex act itself.

Most of them assume that the insertion of the penis into the vagina must be the highlight of the woman's sex life, just as it is for them. But it isn't true. Actually, the most exciting part of the sex act for a woman occurs in the outer "plumbing."

I remember working with a young couple, Gilbert and Ginny, who had been married for more than four years and were having quite a bit of trouble in their marriage, much of it in the area of sex. I asked Gilbert if he exercised great caution and much gentleness when he stroked his wife's clitoris, and his response was, "Her whatsis?"

He didn't even know that his wife had something called the clitoris, but then, she didn't know she had one either! She knew she had some parts "down there" that were more pleasurable than others, but they hadn't spent any time at all talking about their sexual needs. Their sexual union always took place in the dark, in the same room, without any conversation whatsoever. There were no expressions of love, no sweet nothings—just a sterile coming together of two robots. No wonder she said she felt like a "sexual receptacle."

When it comes to sex, it's important to learn the ballpark you're playing in. It's not enough to know your own body, your own limitations, your own pleasurable zones. You also need to find out what excites your mate, and that means being able and willing to tell each other what you like and don't like when it comes to sex.

A man should understand that a woman's clitoris, in contrast to the vagina, which has few nerve endings, is highly sensitive and must be touched in a soft and gentle manner. This will bring great stimulation to a woman in a matter of minutes, but if the man becomes too aggressive, too rough, too strong, or too hurried, most women's systems will automatically shut down.

I think the neatest thing about the clitoris is that it apparently was created for just one reason—to respond. That's the only reason for its existence as far as I have been able to determine. In case I've lost you at this point, the clitoris is located where the folds of the inner lips of the vulva come together. It has dozens of nerve endings, and with indirect or direct stimulation in this area, it fills with blood and becomes erect, much like the male penis. Usually, gently stroking the shaft of the clitoris is immeasurably stimulating for most women—and in fact it is only with gentle stimulation of the clitoral region that a woman is able to reach orgasm.

Now there has been an ugly rumor going around that there are two types of orgasms, one by way of manual stimulation of the clitoral region and the other by insertion of the penis into the vagina. I guess this rumor started because we think it would be ideal for both partners to reach orgasm together during the act of intercourse. However, the input I have received from hundreds of couples tells me that simultaneous orgasms are not common. One person generally reaches orgasm before the other, and usually if the woman is to have one at all, hers must come first. My feeling is that too much emphasis has been placed on the desirability of simultaneous orgasms. The goal for the sexual relationship should be to enjoy each other to the maximum without putting predetermined expectations on the wonderful union. It is unrealistic for a man to expect his wife to respond ultimately every time they have sex. This takes the spontaneity out of sex, and if you're too busy with the rules of the game, you can't enjoy the sport.

Some men become angry or get their feelings hurt if their wives don't reach orgasm every time they have sex, but the truth is that women don't always have to reach orgasm to be satisfied, nor are they likely to reach orgasm every time. Should a husband try to help his wife reach orgasm? Absolutely. But if she doesn't, it may be the case that she was completely satisfied by the closeness of the sexual union, the tenderness and oneness, and the knowledge that she has met the sexual needs of her husband.

Many men grow up thinking that they have to be aggressive, rough-and-tumble. But when it comes to sex, what

235

really counts is gentleness, kindness, caring, and softness. Sex truly does begin early in the day, in the kitchen with a shared cup of coffee, with kind words, with thoughtfulness, with consideration, and with encouraging words and actions.

So men, your wife really wants you to be gentle and soft and caring. Women, what do you suppose men want you to be? You guessed it! Aggressive! It's amazing to me that women are taught to be pink, unassuming, soft, and submissive. Yet we find that when women become sexually aggressive it is very satisfying and stimulating to men.

I remember working with John and Karen, who were both in their middle twenties and had been married for several years. He was a graduate student in the field of electrical engineering. Every night John came home, ate dinner, and then went right to his little desk in the hallway and began to study. Karen would try to initiate conversation, only to be told that he was too busy to talk because he had to get a paper done or complete a project.

So it was that Karen spent most of her nights watching television by herself. She told me that she felt used because the only time John was interested in her was when he had sex on his mind. Other than that, he never told her that he loved her or let her know that he thought she was beautiful. And even those times were becoming less frequent as his schoolwork demanded more and more of his time.

When I asked her where she felt she stood on his list of priorities she said, "At best I'm second. His books and schoolwork are certainly number one."

When I asked her what she was prepared to do about it, she sighed and said, "I've tried putting on sexy nightgowns, complete with my best Estée Lauder perfume, but no results."

I said, "Well, there are times I believe we really have to take the bull by the horns, take things in our own hands.

What you have to do is literally take your husband's genitals into your hands."

She looked shocked at my suggestion, but I went on. "I want you to make the commitment that those books are not going to win. That you are in fact going to get his attention. There's not a husband out there who doesn't want to feel that he's prized, that he's loved. But you need to become aggressive with him."

Her lifestyle was such that being aggressive did not come naturally to her at all. But she made the commitment, after a few more suggestions from me, to greet John at the door one night with a warm kiss, to fight off the probability of his giving her a little peck on the cheek and getting on with his normal routine.

Sure enough, one night he walked in the door and she planted a big kiss on him. She held him so he couldn't get away and began to unbuckle his belt. The poor devil never got beyond the front hall. She took things into her own hands, literally. John later told me that was one of the greatest times they had ever had sexually—because she took action. She committed herself not to be defeated by some inanimate object.

So, women, when your husband comes home from work, let him know right then and there that you are interested in his little body. If you feel like loving, love. Or at least let him know that he is special to you and you would like to be making love to him. A woman can make her husband feel prized and loved by letting him know that she really does want him, or she can make him feel rejected and crummy by turning him down, by emasculating him, and by continually refusing his sexual advances.

And while I'm on the subject, let me say that when you're making love is not the correct time to point out the mistakes your lover is making. "That's all wrong," or "You really fouled that up," are not loving, inspirational words.

Instead, after your time together, discuss what feels good or doesn't. But do it in a loving manner so as to bond you closer together—rather than in a harsh and abrasive way that can lead to hurt feelings.

Men need to hear from their wives that they are on the right track. Rather than being a flaw picker or completely silent in bed, try reinforcing in a positive and loving way those things that are going on that are exciting and pleasurable. Men and women both have a need to know that they are attractive, prized, and special.

I doubt seriously if there is a man alive today who at one time or another hasn't had a fantasy or daydream about his wife meeting him at the door and chasing after him or becoming superaggressive.

I'd like to share with you what happened to me one summer Friday evening. You know how Fridays are. You come home all hot and tired and somewhat worn out by the activities of the week. Your tie is loose and you're ready for dinner. I should have suspected from the beginning that something was up because I didn't see the children in front of the house. They were usually sitting out on the front rocks trying to decide whose turn it was to help me steer the car up the driveway.

When they weren't there, I didn't think much of it, but when I walked into the house I knew something was amiss. The dining-room table was set with the best china (the dishes that don't bounce if you drop them) and the stereo was playing soft music. Attached to the back door was a piece of red yarn, which ran down to a note that was taped to the floor. The note read, "Follow this red string and you'll find a beautiful thing."

So I threw down my clothes . . . er . . . briefcase and began to leisurely follow the red yarn. I followed it into the bathroom where I found another note, which said, "Not here, dummy, try the bed."

Well, sure enough, there was a beautiful thing in the bed—my wife, Sande. She had gone out of her way to let me know how really special I was in her life. You would have to know Sande to appreciate the fact that this sort of thing is not her style, but she did it anyway—including arranging for the children to spend the evening at their grandmother's house.

It is safe to say that all the preparation was just for me. As we talked about it afterward, I shared with her how special she had made me feel. We never did have dinner, and I never found out what happened to her meal, but we had a great time by ourselves.

What a lucky husband I am to have a wife who will go to such extremes to make me feel special and happy. I tell her every day that I love her and that she means everything to me. I don't believe "I love you" is something you can ever say too much or wear out in any relationship. If you love someone, show it and say it. It's the best thing you can do!

# 12

## *Couples of Promise*

Unless you've been living in a cave somewhere, you've heard about Promise Keepers. Maybe you're one of the millions of men who have attended PK events, or you're married to one of them. Then you know how it goes: Hubby hauls off for a weekend with a stadium full of screaming guys, while Wifey stays home with the screaming kids. Nothing new about that—only this time hubby comes back with a new commitment. Suddenly he's helping more with the kids, whispering sweet nothings, pledging his life-long faithfulness. Maybe that's not the story in every home, but in many.

Whenever a popular movement makes the kind of splash that Promise Keepers has made, it means a nerve has been hit. Some deep need is suddenly being met. In this case, men were being delinquent in their promise-keeping—to their wives, to their churches, to God. Even Christian men were being swayed by the "do what feels good" philosophy of our culture. They needed a kick in the pants. (And PK can also stand for Pants Kick.)

Critics have had a field day. "It's just a big pep rally," they say. Well, maybe so—but a lot of guys can use some pep, especially when it comes to keeping promises. "Why aren't women invited?" the critics wonder. Well, women have always been a bit better at keeping promises. Think of Promise Keepers as the remedial class for students with special needs.

It's not my job to defend PK from its attackers, but I think it's time to take their concept to a new level. Now that men are beginning to wake up to the joys of promise-keeping, it's time to reach out to couples. Husbands and wives make promises to each other. *Both* are affected by the selfish spirit of our society. *Both* need encouragement in keeping their vows. Men who've been newly inspired to make their marriages work, women who've suffered from "PK envy," and any of you who *have* been living in caves and missing out on this whole phenomenon—let's all get in on the ground floor of a brand-new emphasis.

Couples of Promise.

I have founded a new movement by that name, and we're holding Couples of Promise conferences around the country, dedicated to improving marriages. I've been pleased to be part of the faculty of Marriage Builders, sponsored by Women of Faith, and we've held conferences in major arenas all over the U.S. and Canada.

But Couples of Promise is something different—a grassroots ministry that empowers couples to teach classes on marriage *in their home churches.* Some of these teachers will join with me in larger seminar settings. We aim to offer practical wisdom, challenging all participants to uphold their marriage vows consistently and creatively. I have also authored a marriage curriculum that many churches are using—*Becoming a Couple of Promise* (Navpress)— and a video series with the same focus—*Keeping the Promise*. And these days what would a new organization be without a web site? Just punch in http://www.couplesof promise.com

I hope you're catching the double meaning of the title "Couples of Promise." Say your daughter takes piano lessons for six months and then performs in a recital. The teacher may say, "She has promise." What does that mean? It means that, although she may sound really bad right now, she is learning the basic skills that will make her a good, even great, pianist someday.

The same thing could be said of your marriage. You may be hitting some clunkers now and then, but if you maintain your commitment to commitment, you'll develop those basic skills that will make your marriage good, even great. You are a couple of promise.

And promises are what it's all about. The bride and groom stand before God and say "I do" to a list of promises. "For richer or poorer, in sickness and in health." The wording of the vows may differ, but there are vows. That's what a marriage is, a promise to be together as you go through life. In biblical language, the two become one. You have been coupled together by the promises you make.

Those promises aren't always easy to keep. If they were, what would be the point of making them? Promises are *meant* for the tough times, the times when she's puking her guts out, when he's got a beer belly, when an old flame calls and hints about reigniting. You keep your promise even when you don't feel like it.

And so couples of promise have a promising future because they're committed to keeping the promises they've made in the past. It's a commitment they have to work at in the present, every day.

## THE TEN COMMITMENTS

But what does this marriage commitment involve? Merely staying together? You probably know some couples that slog through hateful marriages simply because they don't believe in divorce. I appreciate their beliefs, and I share them, but marriage has to be better than that.

A marriage commitment certainly involves sexual fidelity. You can't cheat on your spouse and be true to your marriage; that goes without saying. But there's more than that too.

This book is based on the idea that marriage is a whole-life commitment—not just for the rest of your life but involving the totality of who you are! Sex begins in the kitchen because the way you share the household chores is an integral part of the whole package of love and commitment you have for each other. Properly understood, the marriage vows don't end with "I will not have an affair." They also include "I will not read the paper when you need to talk" . . . "I will not talk to my mother about the private things of our relationship" . . . "I will not tear you down in front of the kids."

Every marriage has many issues like these. The details will differ, but they share some basic principles. I've tried to boil these down to ten. They don't quite have the same power of what Moses brought down from Mount Sinai, but I humbly call them "The Ten Commitments."

1. We commit ourselves to make love a daily choice, even when life looks easier somewhere else.
2. We commit ourselves to treasure each other as gifts from God.
3. We commit ourselves to be quick to forgive and not to hold grudges.
4. We commit ourselves to make time for each other.

5. We commit ourselves to talk daily about our thoughts and feelings.
6. We commit ourselves to show respect for each other publicly and privately, avoiding put-downs, selfish demands, and belittling words.
7. We commit ourselves to try to get behind each other's eyes, to understand the other's specific needs.
8. We commit ourselves to do all we can to make sure our marriage has a positive impact on those around us.
9. We commit ourselves to pray for each other and support each other's spiritual growth.
10. We commit ourselves to honor God and each other through our thoughts, words, and actions.

### COMMITMENT #1

*We commit ourselves to make love a daily choice, even when life looks easier somewhere else.*

Marriage isn't everything it's cracked up to be. It's better.

In fact, researchers tell us that married people are the happiest and healthiest folks on earth. But, like everything of true value, sometimes you have to fight for your marriage. This "two become one" business isn't painless. It takes hard work to make it work. But when it's working, it really hums.

Marriage has no automatic pilot, though. You can't flick a switch and lean back and forget about it. You have to stay at the controls, making adjustments, making it fly. Every day you have to decide to love your mate. Every day.

Temptation takes no holidays. Grab the remote control and flick through a few channels—you're sure to find something that's trying to make you dissatisfied with what you've got. Some hunk or babe with an impossibly pro-

portioned body, forcing you into the comparison game—
"Why don't you look like that, honey?" Some sitcom that
laughs off adultery or laughs at fidelity—"Hmmm, maybe
cheating is no big deal." Some talk show that urges you
to please yourself first and foremost—"Why sacrifice your
life for others?"

Every day you get a million messages promoting the
single life, the sex-filled life, the selfish life. "If only you
weren't tied down in marriage, you too could be having
all this fun." It's tempting to gaze over the fence at all that
green grass, so much greener than yours.

Just remember: If you managed to climb over to that
greener grass, you'd still have to mow it.

Seriously, you need to talk to some real single people,
some real divorced people. Don't buy the ideas of the two-
dimensional images on your TV screen. Talk to flesh-and-
blood people and see how wonderful the single life really
is. The truth is, it's okay sometimes. It can be fun but it
can also be lonely. For every plus involved in the freedom
of non-attachment, there's a minus of not having anyone
to share it with. It's not all parties and piña coladas. Lots
of single people are gazing wistfully over the fence at *your*
lawn.

You, on the other hand, have the privilege of experienc-
ing the miracle of two-becoming-one. It's a sweaty, gritty,
gutsy kind of miracle, but it can be truly amazing. You
can make it truly amazing by working at it every day.
Counter your daily temptation with a daily decision to show
love to your spouse. Instead of being pulled away from
your marriage commitment, take a step toward greater
commitment. Don't even dance with temptation. Flip the
channel. Turn the page. Avert your eyes. Remind yourself of the blessing God has given you in this marriage,
and commit yourself to do the work necessary to make
it really fly.

### COMMITMENT #2

*We commit ourselves to treasure each other as gifts from God.*

A beautiful phrase is engraved inside my wedding ring: "You are my richest blessing." That's how I feel about Sande, and amazingly she feels the same about me. I suppose that, over time, those words are being engraved onto the skin of my ring finger. They're certainly engraved on my heart.

Your spouse is a valuable treasure, a gift to you from the Almighty. How do you treat a treasure?

You know, I've had more than my share of backyard barbecues. And the burgers and potato salad are usually served on what? Paper plates. Some barbecues get really fancy and use those cardboard-like plates, where the sauce won't leak through. Some even have wicker plate holders. In any case, even the finest paper plates are no treasures. They're made to be messed up and thrown away. You can play Frisbee with them, have the dog fetch them, throw them in a bonfire—no one cares!

Now my wife is into antiques. And she has collected a few rare dishes with exquisite craftsmanship and fine materials. How do you think she'd feel if I brought those out for our next barbecue? "Here, Rover, catch!" I have the feeling *I'd* be the one in the doghouse that night.

No, antiques are treasures. You don't put sloppy hamburgers on them. Hey, we don't even use them for our sit-down dinners. They're too valuable for that. We honor their value by displaying them, not tossing them around.

Are you treating your spouse as a paper plate or a rare antique? (And that has nothing to do with your spouse's age, please!) That is, are you honoring your partner as a person of great value, or are you simply using your partner as a convenience, a throwaway item?

(Bill Bennett, former education secretary and author of *The Book of Virtues,* told of attending a wedding where the vows were situational at best. Not "for better or worse"; just "I'll love you as long as love sustains us," or some such nonsense. Bennett says he thought the most appropriate wedding gift for this couple might not be fine china but paper plates.)

"Be devoted to one another in brotherly love," the apostle Paul said. "Honor one another above yourselves" (Rom. 12:10). Of course, he was talking to the whole congregation at Rome, hence the "brotherly" love. I would hope the love in your marriage is more than brotherly. But the apostle's idea can revolutionize the relationship between you and your spouse.

First of all, you're not just committed, you're *devoted*. You may have a child who is totally devoted to something—baseball, horses, computers, a drum set (for your sake, I hope not). Every waking minute is spent thinking about, talking about, or doing something related to that pursuit. That's *devotion*. And if your spouse is a God-given treasure, it makes sense that you'd be just as devoted.

But the apostle's next phrase is even more helpful: "Honor one another above yourselves." You grant honor to someone who is more important than you are. If you go into court to fight that traffic violation (I know you didn't do it, but let's just suppose)—what do you call the judge? "Your Honor." And in a marriage, you have to give your spouse that same respect.

Paul said something similar to the Philippians: "In humility consider others better than yourselves" (Phil. 2:3). What does this look like in a marriage? How does this affect the way you make decisions together? How does it change the way you argue? Who gets to handle the remote control? When you begin to honor your spouse as a treasure from God, everything changes.

These two concepts—devotion and honor—balance each other. Devotion is a passionate thing, but honor is a more practical matter. You can honor your spouse *even when you don't feel like it.* In court, you can feel you've been treated unfairly, but you still call the judge *Your Honor.* And in a marriage you must still honor your spouse. Even if you're in a bad mood, your mate is still a treasure given to you by God.

### COMMITMENT #3

*We commit ourselves to be quick to forgive and not to hold grudges.*

Early in my counseling career, I sat across from a couple who were well past their Medicare years as they finally discovered the freedom of forgiveness. The problems had started thirty years earlier when the husband invited his mother to move in with them. I should explain that this man's leadership was akin to that of General Patton. He didn't ask his wife about this arrangement; he ordered her to get the place ready for Mama.

As you might guess, the wife had a problem with that. But she didn't talk about it, and he didn't ask about it. She just kept the anger within her. Other events occurred over the years that added to her bitterness. But rather than bringing it all out into the open, she just shut down her feelings for her husband. Of course this frustrated him, but he just kept barking orders and nursing his own grudges. And so for thirty years they had a distant, emotionally estranged marriage.

But there in my office that day, she decided to let it all go. She forgave him. And suddenly they were locked in an embrace, tears streaming down both their faces, as they wondered why they hadn't forgiven each other years earlier.

Thirty years! What a waste!

But if you've had any experience with being hurt and trying to forgive, you can see how that might happen. Forgiveness isn't easy. Sometimes it seems better to shove the whole thing under the carpet. But eventually you reach a point where there's more stuff under the carpet than on top of it.

Plentiful research has shown the dangers of holding things in. Your anger will find its way out somehow. It will throw off your internal systems. It will cause pain in your head, neck, back, or stomach. Forgiving is just plain good for you.

But any good discussion on this subject must say what forgiveness is *not*.

Forgiveness is not excusing. It doesn't say, "Oh, that's all right, no problem." On the contrary, it says there *was* a problem, a big problem, that I have to forgive you for.

Forgiveness does not automatically make everything hunky-dory. Hunky, maybe, but the dory will take some time. Seriously, forgiveness does improve a relationship, but it doesn't fix everything. It merely puts you in a place where you can start repairing the damage. The couple embracing in my office that day had taken a huge first step, but there were many steps to go. He still needed to work on his leadership style. She needed to learn how to talk about her feelings.

I'm reminded of the story of Jesus and the adulteress (John 8:1–11). She had been caught in the act and the town leaders were ready to stone her to death. But before they did, they asked Jesus to rule on this case. Should they stone her? The law demanded it.

Jesus played it coy, writing with his finger in the dust of the ground. Then he stood up and said, "If any one of you is without sin, let him be the first to throw a stone at her." Then he bent down and wrote some more. What was he writing? No one knows. I like the idea of some scholars: that he was listing the sins of those leaders.

As it turned out, no one could throw the first stone, and so they left. Jesus was the only one sinless enough to condemn her, and he refused to. "Go," he said to the woman, "and leave your life of sin."

She had experienced lifesaving forgiveness, but now she had the obligation to change her life. In a marriage too, forgiveness should instigate change.

We also learn from this story that forgiveness is not condemnation. I said earlier that forgiveness does not excuse bad behavior; in fact, it shines the spotlight on it. But sometimes the forgivers can seem awfully high and mighty. You don't want to end an argument with "I forgive you for being so stupid about this." That's not true forgiveness. That's a battle cry.

Like the accusers of the adulteress, we must realize that we are a pretty imperfect lot of people. We must forgive others because we want to be forgiven ourselves. What goes around comes around, especially in a marriage. If you start stockpiling grudges, soon you'll have a nasty cold war on your hands.

Let me ask you: How many times have you forgiven your spouse for the same offense? Two? Three? Maybe five? Outrageous, isn't it? But when Jesus was asked how often a person should forgive another, he said, "Seventy times seven." You may feel that you've reached the limit with your spouse, but you probably still have four hundred and eighty-some to go!

Some tell you to forgive and forget. I say forgive and remember. Remember where you were and where you are now, and give thanks that you've moved from point A to point B. Remember enough to change things. But then choose to let go of the pain. Forgiveness is basically a letting go. It's the hardest thing in the world, but it's also one of the simplest. Just let go. Cling to your grudges and you will suffocate your marriage. Take a chance on letting them go and feel the freedom.

### COMMITMENT #4

*We commit ourselves to make time for each other.*

We all have the same amount of time, it's just how we choose to use it. Yes, it's a busy world. You have a zillion things to do. But don't let your spouse get lost in the shuffle. You need to spend time together.

I've already talked about time as a love language. Certain people show their love by spending time with the other person, and they want to receive love in that way. If your spouse has this love language, I'm sure you're already dealing with this issue. But that doesn't let the rest of us off the hook. Even if you have another love language, you still need to spend *some* time together.

Time is money, they say. I think time is becoming even more valuable than money. As our schedules tighten up, it's nearly impossible to squeeze anything else in. And so the way you spend your time is an indication of what's most important to you—even more than how you spend your money. So take a good look at your datebook and measure your priorities. How important is your spouse and your family in relation to everything else you're doing? Do any adjustments need to be made?

People used to talk about "quality time" a lot. They thought they could spend *less* time together as long as it was *better* time. Ten minutes of intense discussion beats two hours of watching TV together. That was the theory. But the fact is, we need *both* quality time and quantity time. We need both intense discussions and relaxing down times.

I know people have demanding jobs, and I know people travel. I'm on the road a lot myself. But thanks to modern technology you can still keep in touch, even if you're halfway across the world. Cell phones and e-mail and FedEx have shrunk the globe, so you can still let your family know how important they are to you.

My second daughter, Kris, recently got her engagement ring. I was out of town at the time, but when I got the news I called back to Tucson and ordered flowers to be delivered to the school where Kris teaches. Well, as you might guess, that made her day.

Even if your busy life carries you away from your family, you must learn to stay involved in their lives. Take the time to connect across the miles by phone, fax, or even flowers.

But at some point you may have to take a long, hard look at your demanding job and ask, "Is this job worth my marriage?" It's a tough decision to make, but I've known a number of people who were glad they ditched a job that kept them away from home long hours. Most of them are making less money now, but their lives are better and their marriages stronger. (And think long and hard before accepting a job that will force you to move away from your extended family, your friends, your church. Even if you're getting a major raise in pay, the loss of these support systems for your spouse and children may not be worth it.)

Not long ago I was invited to speak at some big conference, but it was my daughter's birthday, so I turned them down. The organizer didn't want to take no for an answer, so he kept offering me more and more money. I kept saying no. The sum reached an absurdly high level, and I still didn't take it, though the organizer was dumbfounded. He just didn't get it. What amount of money would compensate me for telling my daughter that she was worth less than a speaking engagement? Even Bill Gates wouldn't have enough to lure me away.

Your marriage is like a plant growing in your garden. There are lots of things you can do to tend it, feed it, help it grow. But if you neglect it, danger arises. Weeds grow. Bugs attack. A host of "marriage eaters" will nip away at your relationship. While you're off on your fishing trip or buried in your computer room, while you're leading that Cub Scout troop or working late, all sorts of frustrations, false expectations, temptations, and sour feelings will threaten your marriage. This doesn't mean you shouldn't do those things; it just means you need to guarantee time together to tend your "marriage plant."

One additional tip: Don't let your kids get involved in everything under the sun. I know you want to develop their talents, but too much activity puts pressure on the whole family timetable. When the family dinner becomes gulp-and-go, when Mom and Dad feel like a limo service, when the whole lot of you are passing like subway trains in the night—that's no way to live. Get your whole family to commit to some quiet family time, and it will be better for all of you. (If this gulp-and-go description hits you squarely between the eyes, you might consider reading two other books I've written, *Bringing Up Kids without Tearing Them Down* and *Becoming the Parent God Wants You to Be*.)

### COMMITMENT #5

*We commit ourselves to talk daily about our thoughts and feelings.*

Every marriage needs a high dosage of Vitamin C. Communication. It's good for you. It builds up your immune system, making you stronger and less susceptible to problems. And just as Vitamin C is a *daily* necessity—your body doesn't store it up—so is communication. You have to talk every day.

You see, you're going to have some disagreements, some misunderstandings, some different priorities. Between the two of you, you'll often have three opinions. I love the quote from Ruth Bell Graham, Billy's wife, when asked if she and her husband always agreed. "My goodness, no!" she said. "If we did, there would be no need for one of us."

Communicating your thoughts and feelings, even when they're in conflict, is a way that the two become one. No, you won't always reach agreement. Often you'll agree to disagree. Marriages are full of negotiation, compromises, and treaties that would make Henry Kissinger proud. But regular communication can eliminate the nasty surprises, secrets, and grudges that bring down many a marriage.

In *HomeLife* magazine, Neil Clark Warren listed "eight secrets to conflict resolution." They serve as a good starting point for any marital communication. Warren's secrets are:

1. Recognize marriage as a "we" business. (You're in it together. Look for a win-win.)
2. Process the data as quickly as possible. (Don't hold back. Get disagreements out in the open.)
3. Stick to the subject.
4. Don't intimidate.
5. No name-calling.
6. Turn up your listening sensitivity. (Make sure you know what the other is really saying.)
7. Practice give and take. (Especially give.)
8. Celebrate every victory. (It's fun to solve a problem together.)[16]

Of course, communication isn't all conflict. Often it's just sharing your feelings about each other or about something you've experienced. Here are some additional tips for nonconflict talking:

*Give time and space to slow sharers.* Some people open up easier than others. (In general, women are more open about their feelings.) Sometimes slow sharers just need some extra time to dredge up their feelings, to identify them, to feel safe talking about them. Give them that time. And offer safety. Don't pounce. Let them word their ideas just right before you respond.

*Relax.* Nothing's more threatening than when one spouse sits the other down and says, "We need to talk." *(Uh-oh, what have I done now?)* If you're in a crisis, then do that, but if this is just your daily conversation, let it flow naturally. Don't try to manufacture it.

*Talk about life around you.* Every day you experience scads of stimuli. Talk about your experiences but also about how you *feel* about those experiences. Work, children, church, TV shows, songs, highway construction—you never have to run out of things to talk about.

*Learn about your mate's passions.* Of course, *you* are your mate's greatest passion (you hope). But don't be afraid to ask about the other things he or she is into. Learn about fly-fishing or macramé, basketball or ballet. Even if you'll never share that passion, you can at least appreciate it.

*Ask penetrating questions but don't interrogate.* Always be ready to plunge into the next deepest level of conversation. For instance, if your spouse is recounting the events of the working day, you could ask, "How do you feel about what happened?" But if your spouse doesn't want to take that plunge, ease up. You're not working for the FBI.

*Instead of asking "Why?" learn to say, "Tell me more about that."* The question Why? is a challenge that often puts the recipient on the defensive. Indicate your interest without demanding an explanation.

*Listen as much as you speak.* Be sure there's a balance between you in your speaking time. And really listen—don't just rehearse what you're going to say next.

### COMMITMENT #6

*We commit ourselves to show respect for each other publicly and privately, avoiding put-downs, selfish demands, and belittling words.*

Once I knew a great guy with a terrible temper. He was a pillar of his church, making extremely generous financial contributions. He supported missionaries to the hilt, buying whatever they needed. Clearly this was a mighty man of God—except for that temper.

His wife had a heart for people too. She was very sweet, perhaps too sweet, because his angry outbursts destroyed her. And she frequently bore the brunt of his rage. One minute he'd be advising church leaders on some matter of ministry, and the next minute his hair-trigger temper would erupt. He would berate his wife in public for some little thing. It was embarrassing for everybody.

Public put-downs are a no-no for any marriage. Private criticism is bad enough, but when one spouse berates the other in front of friends and neighbors, that's especially damaging. And yet many couples do this! Maybe they think they'll get support from their "audience." Or maybe they just really want to embarrass their partner, but they wind up embarrassing themselves.

Sometimes when "the boys" or "the girls" get together, they'll think it's funny to complain about their spouses. If the complaints are mild, this is fine, even healthy. These occasions can serve as support groups. But every so often, the comments turn ugly. A wife finds herself constantly bad-mouthing her husband in front of her friends. The husband unloads frustrations he really ought to take up with her.

It's quite a different picture we find in Proverbs 31, where the husband praises the wife publicly, saying: "Many women do noble things, but you surpass them all" (v. 29). On the other hand, the wife "brings him good, not harm, all the days of her life" (v. 12), and "her husband is respected at the city gate" (v. 23), no doubt because his wife isn't telling everyone what a fool he is. I just love to hear husbands and wives speak well of each other in public. It indicates a genuine respect within their marriage.

But even in private, you must be careful about the damaging power of words. You will have legitimate criticisms from time to time, but "speak the truth in love." Look for positive things to say that can balance out the negative things. Be honest about your disagreements, but don't belabor the point. If there's something painful your spouse needs to hear, I favor a hit-and-run technique—make your point, assure them of your undying love, and back off. Don't beat them over the head. An explosion on your part may make *you* feel better in the short term, but it might just set off a time bomb within your spouse and you'll feel the heat yourself in a few days.

Sometimes problems can inflate like a balloon. If you keep blowing up a balloon, you'll reach a point where it's about to burst. One more tiny breath will cause an explosion. And I've seen some marriages like that, just about to burst. But if you take that balloon, squeeze the neck and let just a little air out, the situation eases. It's no longer at a bursting point.

That's why Commitment #5 goes with Commitment #6. You have to talk daily about the issues of your life together so things don't inflate to the bursting point. But if they do, ease out of the problem gently, using words that build rather than destroy.

### COMMITMENT #7

*We commit ourselves to try to get behind each other's eyes, to understand the other's specific needs.*

I've already discussed "his needs" and "her needs" and the importance of "getting behind your spouse's eyes." So let me just tell you a story.

I was on a business trip in Erie, Pennsylvania, and I wanted to buy my wife a little something. I'm not much of a gift-giver—I mean, I don't always bring home a gift every time I go away—but this time I wanted to get her something personal. So I walked into a mall and stumbled upon this store called Victoria's Secret. It was the first time I'd ever walked into this place, and I must have looked like I just fell off the turnip truck. I remember walking in, shuffling my feet, saying, "Shazam!" As I sidled along, I nearly knocked over a mannequin, which was dressed in a scanty little outfit, and I about died. I mean, mannequins today look very real.

Then not one but *two* clerks came out—young kids, young enough to be my own children. This one little girl came up and said, at about 40 decibels, "HI, SIR! HOW ARE YOU TODAY? LOOKING FOR SOME BRAS? MAYBE SOME PANTIES?"

I quickly walked into a corner and said very softly, "Listen, lady, I'm just looking for a nightie."

Of course she went back to 40 decibels again. "OH, WE'VE GOT ALL KINDS OF NIGHTIES. COME ON OVER HERE."

So she pulled this nightie off the rack and held it up. I'm not kidding—it was about a foot-and-a-half long at best. And I just looked at her, shaking my head. "No, this will never do. My wife is 5-foot-9 inches tall not 2-foot-9 inches tall."

But that did not deter this young lass from anything. She went back to the rack and grabbed another nightie, a long, red one with spaghetti straps over the shoulder. (I'm colorblind, so I didn't know what color it was.) It ended up costing me ninety bucks. It was silk.

So the woman wrapped it up, not tucked away in a box but in a Victoria's Secret bag, with crinkly paper on top. In the meantime the other girl sold me three jars of stuff to rub on your body that's supposed to smell good, and those cost ten bucks each, so now I'd spent ninety bucks plus thirty bucks. I was out 120 bucks and I had a little package in my hand. And, to tell you the truth, I felt a bit stupid.

I got home a day later. Sande was still up, reading the paper at the kitchen table. I plunked the package down in front of her. "What's that?" she asked.

"Oh, just a little something."

"Oh, you're so sweet," Sande responded, giving me a little peck. And she opened it and said, "Oh, honey, it's beautiful!" And she went to hang it up.

I never saw that nightie again.

All of this happened when I was 50 years old. I had written fifteen books by that time, and I knew something about women and men. I certainly knew Sande, and I should have known the kind of nightie Sande likes. Well, right now she's got a plaid one with legs in it. Her favorites are flannel—5/8" thick. I've got plywood in my garage that's not that thick.

So I don't know what she did with the red silk nightie. Maybe she gave it to the poor. Some guy's probably checking his oil with it tonight on the south side of Tucson.

Anyway, whose eyes was I behind when I bought that nightie? My own. I wanted to buy her something special, but I didn't stop to think about what would be special for *her*. Spouses often do that when they should know better. I've bought my wife a lot of stupid gifts over the years, and she's bought me some stupid ones too. But the best gift you can give is to get behind his or her eyes, to understand what your partner really wants and needs.

### COMMITMENT #8

*We commit ourselves to do all we can to make sure our marriage has a positive impact on those around us.*

We are not alone. We're being watched. Many eyes are following the day-to-day events of our marriages.

Sounds like an episode of *The X Files,* doesn't it? Well, relax. I'm not talking about aliens or FBI agents. I'm talking about your children, your relatives, your friends, your neighbors. Your marriage has a profound impact on those around you, like it or not. How are you going to ensure that the impact is good?

Several years ago, basketball star Charles Barkley made headlines by proclaiming, "I am not a role model." He had a point. Why should kids look up to a guy simply because he can throw a ball in a hoop? But the fact is, basketball stars *are* role models for millions of kids. Good or bad, these stars attract the spotlight. Maybe their behavior *shouldn't* be emulated, but it is. So whenever Barkley gets in a bar fight, kids are watching. Whenever a player chokes his coach or gets arrested for drug possession or drives while he's drunk, he has a negative impact on the larger community.

You're a role model too. If you have children, that's where it starts. They're watching you with eagle eyes, and they're taking mental notes. What are they learning about love, about commitment, about marriage?

We have a generation of young adults now who are terrified of commitment because half of them saw their parents divorce. What have they learned from their parents? When the Bible says that God punishes children "for the sin of the fathers to the third and fourth generation" (Exod. 20:5), I think this is the idea behind it. One generation learns from the previous one and passes on its learning to the next.

I've seen it time and time again in my office, as I counsel people who are struggling with images of marriage they've learned from their parents—how Mom treated Dad, how Dad treated Mom. These patterns are reworked in their own relationships.

There are plenty of negative examples in our society, but I know some families that are setting positive patterns too. A strong marriage sends a strong signal to children. As they hear their parents speaking positively about one another and about marriage in general, they will be motivated to adopt those positive patterns.

That verse I quoted about God punishing sin to the third and fourth generation has a sequel. In the next verse God says he shows "love to a thousand generations of those who love me and keep my commandments" (Exod. 20:6). Yes, *positive* patterns of marriage and parenting get passed on and on and on.

Children aren't the only ones watching you. Your marriage also has an impact on your friends and neighbors. If your sister and brother-in-law are having trouble, they may look at you and decide they can get through it. The young man in your church who's afraid to propose to his longtime girlfriend because he comes from a broken home—well, he may see your relationship and decide marriage isn't so bad after all. Strong marriages inspire other strong marriages. You may be providing encouragement to others without even knowing it.

How can you make sure your marriage has a positive impact?

*Let your children know Mom and Dad are crazy about each other.* (They already think you're crazy.) Don't hide your smooching and hugging. Say good things about each other in front of the kids.

*Never use your children as pawns in your disputes.* Don't force them to take sides. No matter how angry you are, don't badmouth your spouse in front of the kids. You want them to retain respect for both of you—even if you're going through a problem.

*Speak often about the joys of marriage.* These days there are plenty of voices mocking marriage. Offer a second opinion, not only in your home but also in your church and community.

*Don't air your dirty laundry.* You don't need to be ultra-secretive, but treat your occasional conflicts as private matters that will be worked out. Don't let the whole world know what an ignoramus your spouse is.

*Offer counsel to younger couples who want it.* Don't go blabbing advice without being asked. That's a good way to lose friends. But let people know that you care, that you'll listen to their problems without judging them harshly, that you may have some experience to share. You don't need to set yourself up as a world expert on marriage, but you've been there. You can certainly share some wisdom. (In fact, this is a basic premise behind our Couples of Promise program. It's not just me telling everyone else how to live; it's local couples sharing what they've learned.)

### COMMITMENT #9

*We commit ourselves to pray for each other and support each other's spiritual growth.*

"These people are just absolutely killing me," Pastor Ron told me over lunch. He had a great heart for the people of his church. He would do anything they needed. When a single mother needed help with her two boys, Ron took them fishing. Ron was constantly counseling, visiting, lending a hand. He was always there for other people—but he neglected his wife.

I've seen this many times among pastors. They're sold out to God, but their wives and children don't matter. Often the wives drift away, emotionally, spiritually. They get bitter about the ministry. They blame God for stealing their husbands. Their spiritual growth gets stunted.

Ironic that a pastor can be so dedicated to enhancing spiritual growth in a congregation and completely ignore it in his own home. Ironic and sad.

Now you may not be a pastor, but you have a ministry to your own husband or wife. How can you help your mate grow spiritually? Of course your spouse is helping you grow too. How can you both develop this mutual growth?

*Pray together.* Get into habits of mutual prayer. At dinnertime, bedtime, in a phone call during the day. You don't need to make it long and religious-sounding, but get used to greeting God as a couple.

*Keep it simple.* You may want to study Scripture together, but don't preach to each other. "Too often we try to model our devotional lives like a Sunday school class or church service," says speaker Steve Davidson. "Simplicity is the key."[17]

*Encourage.* When I came home from the first Couples of Promise conference, Sande showered me with encouragement, telling me what a great job I did. It meant a lot to me. The conference was a major undertaking and I was hoping it would go well. Sande's supportive words were golden. Find ways to encourage your mate in their work, their ministry, and in their spiritual lives. If you've been noticing more patience or humility or joy, say so!

*Challenge.* There's a fine line between challenging and bullying (or nagging). If you stay on the right side of that line, you can nudge your spouse forward in spiritual matters. "Let us consider how we may spur one another on toward love and good deeds," the Bible says (Heb. 10:24). Spurs are sharp but they don't dig too deep. Urge your mate to try some new things, to take some spiritual chances, to become more intentional about spiritual growth. And expect your mate to urge you in the same way.

*Give space.* Your spouse will not grow at the same pace you do. Don't insist on that. Give freedom to your spouse to be the person he or she wants to be. Recognize your differences. This is a mistake many church leaders make: They expect their spouses to be at the same place (of leadership) they are. When the spouses reveal basic doubts or questions, it becomes scandalous, but it shouldn't. Each person should be able to grow at his or her own pace. Encourage, challenge, but then let the growth happen.

### COMMITMENT #10

*We commit ourselves to honor God and each other through our thoughts, words, and actions.*

When Jesus was asked to name the greatest commandment in all the Jewish law, he picked two. The first was (in my own paraphrase): "Love God with all you've got." Heart, mind, strength, soul—pack it all up and send it in his direction. Live your whole life, every aspect of your life, in utter devotion to the One who made you.

That means you should love God with your marriage.

The second commandment was: "Love your neighbor as yourself." This applies to everyone around you—Good Samaritans and bad hombres, the folks next door and the kids who hang out in front of 7-Eleven—treat them all with the same honor you'd want for yourself.

Of course your closest "neighbor" is your spouse. You get no exemption here. You need to love your spouse as you love yourself. In fact, elsewhere the Bible speaks of an intertwining of selves in marriage—a husband should treat his wife's body as his own, and vice versa (1 Cor. 7:4; Eph. 5:28). The two are one flesh.

I've talked about "honor" before. Honor is simply love in action. Honor God with all you've got. Honor each other as you want to be honored. Jesus' two commandments nicely sum up our Ten Commitments.

## BATTLE TO BLESSING

In the past generation a lot of Christian couples have gotten themselves hung up in the whole "battle of the sexes." Torn by traditional scriptural interpretation on one hand and modern liberation on the other, they don't know what to do. Home life becomes an endless episode of "Who's the Boss?"—except it's not funny.

In closing this book, I urge you to get beyond the battle and discover the blessing God intends for marriage. When you read all the pertinent Scriptures, you can't help but get the feeling that we've been missing the point. The question is not "Who will be the boss?" but "How can we serve each other?"

Peter writes, "Husbands, in the same way be considerate as you live with your wives, and treat them with respect as the weaker partner and as heirs with you of the gracious gift of life, so that nothing will hinder your prayers" (1 Peter 3:7).

Lots of women don't like that "weaker partner" business, but let me suggest that the key words are *respect* and *heirs*. Even though wives may be physically weaker and have less pull in society (which was certainly the case in Peter's day and sometimes in our own), husbands must *treat them with respect*. What's more, all of us—men and women alike—share equally in the bounteous blessings of God.

In Ephesians Paul writes, "Submit to one another out of reverence for Christ" (5:21), and he goes on to explain how this is done—beginning with wives and husbands. "Wives, submit to your husbands as to the Lord. . . . Husbands, love your wives, just as Christ loved the church and gave himself up for her" (Eph. 5:22, 25).

Now I know people have all sorts of problems with *submission* and *headship,* but let me suggest that the whole point of this text is *how we serve each other.* Does it really matter who submits more to the other one? Jesus gave us the model of servanthood, giving himself up for us. Both husbands and wives must practice humble service in their daily lives.

I've heard many sermons (usually on Mother's Day) about "the Proverbs 31 woman." Check out that passage and you'll find a Supermom—doing the laundry, driving the kids to soccer practice, and running her own multi-national corporation. No wonder her husband and children "rise up to call her blessed."

But let me give you the picture of "the Genesis 2 woman."

"Then the LORD God made a woman from the rib he had taken out of the man, and he brought her to the man" (v. 22).

I'm told that the Hebrew word for "rib" can mean "side." Clearly this woman is no minor accessory; she is a chunk of Adam, the other half of his flesh.

"The man said, 'This is now bone of my bones and flesh of my flesh; she shall be called "woman," for she was taken out of man'" (v. 23).

I'd like to think that, when he first laid eyes on this exquisite new creation, Adam said something like, "GOL-LEEEEE!!!" Then when he caught his breath, he said the bone and flesh stuff. Obviously this guy is excited.

"For this reason a man will leave his father and mother and be united to his wife, and they will become one flesh" (v. 24).

Two become one; that's the story. Woman is the other half of man. We need each other. Let's stop doing battle and learn to serve. Let's discover all the blessings God has for us. Then we will truly be "couples of promise."

# *Notes*

1. Larry L. Halter, Ph.D., *Traits of a Happy Couple* (Waco, Tex.: Word, 1988), 49–57.

2. Ibid., 214–15.

3. John Powell, *Why Am I Afraid to Tell You Who I Am?* (Niles, Ill.: Argus Communications, 1969).

4. H. Norman Wright, *The Pillars of Marriage* (Ventura, Calif.: Regal, 1979), 156–57.

5. Willard F. Harley, Jr., *His Needs, Her Needs* (Grand Rapids: Fleming H. Revell, 1994).

6. Gary Chapman, *The Five Love Languages* (Chicago: Northfield Publishing, 1995), 48.

7. Ibid., 60.

8. Ibid., 75.

9. H. Norman Wright, *Communication: Key to Your Marriage* (Ventura, Calif.: Regal, 1974), 87–92.

10. David Augsburger, *Caring Enough to Confront* (Ventura, Calif.: Regal, 1973), 46.

11. David Augsburger, *Be All You Can Be* (Carol Stream, Ill.: Creation House, 1970), 31–32.

12. Jay Kesler, *Too Big to Spank* (Ventura, Calif.: Regal, 1978), 66–67.

13. Halter, *Traits of a Happy Couple,* 93–95.

14. Ibid., 94.

15. Letha Scanzoni, *Sex Is a Parent Affair* (Ventura, Calif.: Regal, 1973), 44–45.

16. Neil Clark Warren, "Battlefields and Playgrounds: How to Fight Fair and Make the Good Times Roll," *HomeLife,* October 1998, 20–24.

17. Quoted in "Invite a Marriage Expert to Dinner or Read This Article Instead," by Tricia Goyer, *HomeLife,* October 1998, 29.

# Other Resources by Dr. Kevin Leman

*Videos*
How to Get Kids to Do What You Want
Living in a Stepfamily
Raising Successful and Confident Kids
Why Kids Misbehave

RealFAMILIES Video Club—Teaching tapes with Dr. Kevin
   Leman and Dr. Jay Passavant—call (888) 824-2020 for more
   information.

*Poster*
"A Child's Ten Commandments to Parents"

*Audiotapes*
Sex Begins in the Kitchen
The Deception of Perfection
Raising Successful and Confident Kids
How to Get Kids to Do What You Want Them to Do
How to Be a Healthy Authority over Your Child
Why Kids Misbehave and What to Do about It
How to Make Your Child Feel Special
The Powerful Secrets of Reality Discipline
Keeping Your Family Together When the World Is Falling Apart
Living in a Stepfamily without Getting Stepped On
The Original Designer Genes
God's Design for Marriage
The Submission Mission
"What's Wrong?" . . . "Oh, Nothing"
Her Needs and His
How to Affair-Proof Your Marriage
A Marriage That's Great for Your Kids

**Dr. Kevin Leman** is an internationally known psychologist, author, radio and television personality, and speaker. He has appeared on such television shows as *Oprah, CNN, Leeza, Live with Regis and Kathie Lee, CBS This Morning,* and *The Today Show.* He has served as a consulting family psychologist for *Good Morning America.*

Dr. Leman is also the host of the new syndicated television program, *RealFAMILIES.* He has made house calls for *Focus on the Family, Midday Connection, The 700 Club,* and *Open House.* He is the founder and president of *Couples of Promise.*

The author of numerous books including *The New Birth Order Book, Becoming a Couple of Promise, Making Children Mind without Losing Yours, When Your Best Is Not Good Enough,* and *What a Difference a Daddy Makes,* Dr. Leman is also a husband and the father of five children. He earned his master's and doctorate degrees from the University of Arizona in Tucson, where he and his wife, Sande, now live with their family.

For additional resources, or for seminar information, please contact:

Dr. Kevin Leman
Couples of Promise
P.O. Box 35370
Tucson, Arizona 85704
Phone: (520) 797-3830
fax: (520) 797-3809
Website: www.couplesofpromise.com